Praise for
Meeting God at The Shack

"In this moving book, John Mark Hicks becomes our vulnerable guide on the path of spiritual recovery. He leads us not just through *The Shack*, but also through the exploration of our own 'shacks,' as we seek to believe—all the way to our bones!—that despite our doubts, our failures, our brokenness, God's love for us is unwavering."

    —**Mike Cope,** Director of Ministry Outreach, Pepperdine University

"Beautiful story. You are a clear glass window, brother, and being clear glass is what discipleship is all about."

    —**Scot McKnight,** Julius R. Mantey Professor of New Testament, Northern Seminary

"John Mark shows us the sort of vulnerability and transparency that is central to spiritual health. His personal journey shared with such candor will minister to many others by modeling—and giving permission for them to embrace—the sort of authenticity that allows growth through pain and healing through brokenness."

    —**Rubel Shelley,** author of *I Knew Jesus before He Was a Christian . . . And I Liked Him Better Then*

Meeting
GOD
at *The Shack*

Meeting
GOD
at *The Shack*

A JOURNEY INTO
Spiritual Recovery

John Mark Hicks

LEAFWOOD
PUBLISHERS
an imprint of Abilene Christian University Press

MEETING GOD AT *THE SHACK*

A Journey into Spiritual Recovery

LEAFWOOD
P U B L I S H E R S
an imprint of Abilene Christian University Press

Copyright © 2017 by John Mark Hicks

ISBN 978-0-89112-591-4 | LCCN 2016039574

Printed in the United States of America

Scripture quotations, unless otherwise noted, are from The Holy Bible, New International Version®, NIV®. Copyright © 1973, 1978, 1984, 2011 by Biblica, Inc.® Used by permission. All rights reserved worldwide.

Quotations of *The Shack* are from William Paul Young (in collaboration with Wayne Jacobsen and Brad Cummings), *The Shack: Where Tragedy Confronts Eternity* (Newbury Park, CA: Windblown Media, 2007).

LIBRARY OF CONGRESS CATALOGING-IN-PUBLICATION DATA
Names: Hicks, John Mark, author.
Title: Meeting God at The shack : a journey into spiritual recovery / by John Mark Hicks.
Other titles: Journey into spiritual recovery
Description: Abilene, Texas : Leafwood Publishers, 2017.
Identifiers: LCCN 2016039574 | ISBN 9780891125914 (pbk.)
Subjects: LCSH: Young, William P. Shack. | God in literature. | Spirituality in literature. | Trust in God. | Mental healing.
Classification: LCC PR9199.4.Y696 S5335 2017 | DDC 813/.6—dc23
LC record available at https://lccn.loc.gov/2016039574

Cover design by Marc Whitaker, MTWdesign
Interior text design by Sandy Armstrong, Strong Design

Leafwood Publishers is an imprint of Abilene Christian University Press
ACU Box 29138
Abilene, Texas 79699

1-877-816-4455
www.leafwoodpublishers.com

17 18 19 20 21 22 23 / 7 6 5 4 3 2 1

In 2008 and 2009, many showered their love upon me . . .

my employers—
    both Lipscomb University and Harding School of
    Theology
my counselors—
    I have learned much about myself with your help
my church—
    Woodmont Hills Family of God in Nashville, Tennessee
my Bible classes—
    at Woodmont Hills, who walked with me gracefully
my men's groups—
    where I continue to learn and practice intimacy
my spiritual-care team
    —God's gift to Jennifer and myself
my small group—
    you are all such a joy to me
my brothers and sisters
    —Mack, Sue, Jack, and sister-in-law Melanie
my nieces and nephews—
    Allison, Brittney, Ian, Carson, Logan
my mom—
    you love me no matter what
my daughters—
    Ashley and Rachel, both faithful and loving
my wife, Jennifer—
    for whose steadfast love I am deeply grateful and
    without whom I would not be able to share my story
    in this book

*They have embraced me, and through them, God has loved
me profoundly.*

Thank you!

Contents

Introduction: The Literary Genre of *The Shack*

Part I: Looking Life in the Eye

Part II: Encountering God in a Fresh Way

Conclusion: The Heart of Spiritual Recovery

Warning

I suggest you read *The Shack* before you read this book, because in the pages just ahead I assume that you know the plot and have read the book. I do not want to spoil your experience of reading the novel for the first time.

But, after reading this book, read *The Shack* again. Open yourself up to the spiritual recovery, growth, and development God's Spirit may work in your life toward the Grand Purpose for which God created and redeemed us.

Preface

A broken and contrite spirit,
O God, you will not despise.

Psalm 51:17

William P. Young's *The Shack* became a national best-seller in 2008. As of July 2009 it had sold 7.2 million copies. It remained on the *New York Times* Best Sellers list for more than a year. More importantly, it has touched the hearts of many hurting people. At the same time, Young's book has been the object of hostile attacks from those who believe the novel undermines Christian orthodoxy.

I read the book at the end of January 2008. Moved to tears several times, I was emotionally and intellectually engaged by Young's storytelling. This modern parable addresses some of the most perplexing topics of Christian theology as well as some of humanity's most gut-wrenching experiences. Writing about Trinity (God as three and one), atonement (why did Jesus die?), providence (how God works in the world), suffering, theodicy (can God justify evil?), death of children, parental abuse, forgiving murderers, forgiving self, forgiving God, and incarnation (is Jesus both God and human?) is difficult prose to write, even more difficult to describe in a novel. Such an ambitious task is either foolhardy or courageous but nevertheless at least interesting and intriguing. I found it compelling.

As the book emerged as a phenomenon, several asked me to review it and comment on some of the theological controversy surrounding it. Since I had experienced hurt and pain similar to what the novel describes and had prayed, reflected, taught (in churches and academia), and written about that pain, some thought perhaps I might have something helpful to say about how to read this novel. I have hesitated for several reasons.

I read the book on the verge of my own crisis. I would confront some of my own "demons" in the first weeks of February 2008. I entered a period of rest from ministry and academia just after reading Young's work. Sometimes I wonder if the book even contributed to the timing of my own "shack" as it introduced me to recovery ideas. In any event, I did not want to rush into the blogosphere or into print about the story. I needed time to process my own stuff without focusing on Young's "shack."

Also, I was rather uninterested in the theological controversy swirling around the book. I did not want to engage in any theological debates, nuances, or heresy trials. I did not want to spend time parsing the meaning and specifics of parabolic descriptions and dialogue as if in a heated religious or academic debate. Ultimately, I came to believe the novel had a much more important significance than those disputes.

Further, the subjects Young discusses are close to my own story, heart, and study. Some of the story was too painful to discuss early on. Some of it was too ambiguous (as it seemed at first reading) to pursue with any profit. I needed to work through my own "shack" before engaging Young's parable.

Toward the end of 2008, I changed my mind. The previous several months of my own recovery prepared me to read Young's work again but this time more empathetically. I am still rather uninterested in the theological debates, since I find most of them to be picky and distortions of Young's intent. Instead, I am interested in the spiritual therapy, recovery, and healing available through the book as God's Spirit uses it for such.

I turned my attention to Young's novel after I received a request to lecture on it near the end of September 2008. I was asked to substitute for a speaker who was scheduled to speak on *The Shack* at the 2008 Zoe Conference in Nashville, Tennessee. I had not spoken anywhere since the first weekend of February. I did not intend to speak anywhere for the rest of 2008, other than in a Bible class at the Woodmont Hills Family of God in Nashville beginning that November. However, this invitation seemed like God's timing.

As my wife, Jennifer, and I talked about the possibility, it became clear to us that perhaps this was a moment designed by God for my sake. We discerned that this is about what God wants to do in my "shack." It would give me an opportunity to reflect in a focused way on my own story in the light of Young's parable and metaphors. In other words, I agreed to speak for my own sake more than any other motive.

I had lots of anxiety about speaking, particularly on the emotional subjects that *The Shack* raises. But Jennifer, my spiritual advisors, and I felt it was time, and this was an opportunity practically (more accurately, divinely) tailored for me. I felt called to speak again at that moment at that time on that subject.

So, I read *The Shack* again. It was a different experience for two reasons. First, I listened to Paul Young talk about his own story. This is available in many formats on the Internet from webcasts to podcasts. Any part of his story I tell in this book is derived from his own public words available through the Internet. Second, this time I heard the language of spiritual recovery since I now had ears to hear due to my own journey into emotional, spiritual, and psychological healing.

Consequently, my engagement with *The Shack* does not begin with the controversial questions for which the book has been attacked. Some of them are good questions—goddess worship? open theism? modalism? (some readers are even now saying "huh?")—but they are marginal to my concerns as a griever and a recovering addict. And we are all addicts—sin itself is an addiction before which we are powerless on our own (Rom. 7), and we all express our brokenness in some form of specific powerlessness—overeating, shopping, sex, alcohol, drugs, materialism, work, busyness, television, video games, and so on. Reading *The Shack* as a wounded person, as an addict, is much more important than wrestling with the theological questions it raises.

The first part of this book discusses spiritual recovery, while the second part addresses some of the theological questions that concern many. But even in the second part I am much more interested in how this parable and the theological questions it raises offer an entrance into the substantial themes of divine love, forgiveness, healing, and hope. These are the main concerns of the book.

I think the question the novel addresses is this:

How do wounded people come to believe God deeply loves them?

Reading the book through this lens enables us to understand how Young uses some rather unconventional metaphors to deepen his point.

My interest is to unfold the story of recovery in *The Shack* as I experienced it through my own journey. So, I invite you to walk with me through the maze of grief, hurt, and pain as we, through experiencing Mackenzie's shack, face our own "shacks."

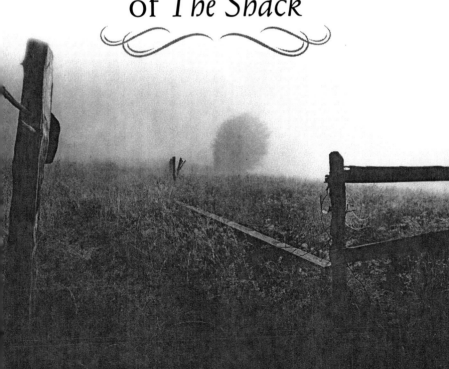

The Literary GENRE

of *The Shack*

CHAPTER 1

What Kind of Book Is *The Shack?*

I will open my mouth with a parable,
I utter hidden things, things from of old.

PSALM 78:2

While some have perhaps read *The Shack* as an actual account, the title page identifies the piece as a *novel*. This is a fictional story. But it is nevertheless true.

When Paul Young talks about his book, he identifies it as an extended modern parable. Like a parable, the events described are fictional though possible (that is, it is not science fiction). And, like a parable, it becomes a world into which we step to hear something true about God, life, and the soul.

The Prodigal Son (Luke 15), for example, is a fictional but true story. As fiction, the story has no correspondence in fact;

that is, it is not a story about a specific, actual family. No one walked up to Jesus after the parable to ask the name of the son, which family he came from, and into which "far country" he went. Whether it is actual history or not is irrelevant. It is a fictional tale. But the story is nevertheless true. The Prodigal Son says something true about God and God's relationship with others.

A parabolic story draws the listener or reader into the world of the parable to see something from a particular angle. A parable is not comprehensive theology but a story-shaped way of saying a particular thing. As a piece of art rather than didactic prose, it allows a person to hear that point in an emotional as well as intellectual way. It gives us imagery, metaphor, and pictures to envision the truth rather than merely describing it in prose. Rather than analyzing propositions, we become part of a parable's narrative. We are free to experience our own life again as we are guided by the storyteller.

Parables, as the parables of Jesus often do, sucker-punch us when we begin to see something we had not previously seen about ourselves, God, or the world. They speak to us emotionally in ways that pure prose does not usually do, much like music, art, and poetry are expressive in ways that transcend discursive or academic descriptions. This enables the right side (the artsy side) of our brain to connect with what the left side (the analytical side) of our brain thinks. We can feel these truths rather than simply think about them. As a result, those truths can connect with our gut (our core beliefs about ourselves) in ways our intellect cannot. The truths, then, can settle into our hearts as well as our minds.

The Shack is, I think, a piece of serious theological reflection in parabolic form. It is not a systematic theology. It does not cover every possible topic nor reflect on God from every potential angle. That is not its intent. That would be too much to expect from a parable or even from any single book. The Prodigal Son, for example, is not a comprehensive teaching about God.

Rather, the focus of *The Shack* is somewhat narrow. Fundamentally, given my own experience and after hearing Young talk about his intent, I read the book as answering this question: *How do wounded people journey through their hurt to truly believe in their gut that God really loves them despite the condition of their "shack"?*

The parable is about how we feel about ourselves in our own "shacks." Do we really believe—deep in our guts, not just in our heads—that God deeply loves us? How can God love us when our "shacks" are a mess? The parable addresses these feelings, self-images, and the soul's wounds.

The theology of *The Shack* engages us at this level. It encourages us to embrace the loving relationship into which God invites us. Consequently, it does not answer every question, address every aspect of God's nature, or reflect on every topic of Christian theology. Instead, it zeroes in on the fundamental way in which wounded souls erect barriers that muzzle the divine invitation to loving relationship.

When reading *The Shack* as serious theological reflection, it is important to keep two points in mind. First, Young wrote the story to share with his kids his own journey into spiritual recovery. His family recognizes he is "Mack," that Missy is his own lost childhood, and Mack's encounter with God over a weekend is a telescoped parable of his own ten-year journey to find healing. It is a story into which Young's children could enter to understand their father's journey from tragedy to hope, from barrenness to relationship with God.

Second, it is serious theology because he shares a vision of God that is at the root of his healing. The parable teaches truth—the truth he came to believe through the process of his own recovery and healing. The "truth," however, is not that God is an African American woman (a metaphor that has angered some). That is simply a parabolic form. Rather, the truth is that God deeply loves Mack despite his "shack" (his "stuff").

This message, once it found a publisher, became available for others beyond his children. It has now become a parable for other readers, and Young invites us to see that the truth he discovered in his own recovery is true for every one of us. God cares for each of us no matter what the condition of our "shacks."

In the following brief chapters, I will use Young's parable as an occasion for thinking about some significant themes in spiritual recovery. *The Shack* will provide the fodder, but I will not limit myself to Young's book in developing the themes. Using the novel as a starting place, I will pursue these themes in the context of my own spiritual journey as well as place them within the Story of God as told in Scripture.

While one aspect of my purpose is to discern whether *The Shack* deserves the hostility some have unleashed upon it, my larger intent is to reflect on spiritual recovery in the context of my own journey to find healing. We will walk alongside Mack as he receives a vision of God that wounded people need and want to hear—a vision available in Scripture itself.

I invite you to reflect on these themes with me—to process them within your own journey, out of your own wounds, and in relationship with your own God.

PART I

Looking Life
IN THE EYE

Entering Our Shacks

CHAPTER 2

What Is the Shack?

Mackenzie,
It's been a while. I've missed you.
I'll be at the shack next weekend if you
want to get together there.

PAPA

When God first invited Mack to the shack (p. 18), his gut feeling was nausea, but it quickly turned to anger. He had always tried to avoid thinking about the shack. He never went to the shack. He insulated himself from it in every way. Except in the vaguest forms, he did not even talk about the shack with others, including his wife, Nan.

The shack created turmoil in the pit of Mack's stomach. The shack was a dead and empty place; it had a twisted, evil face. It was a metaphor for emptiness, unanswered questions, and far-flung accusations against God.

Yet, God wants to meet Mack at the shack.

"Why *the shack*—the icon of his deepest pain?" Mack rages in his inner thoughts. "Certainly God would have better places to meet him?" (67).

The shack, metaphorically, is Mack's own wounded soul, his hurt. It is where Mack keeps his secrets, his hidden thoughts, and he does not let anyone—even his wife, Nan—into his shack.

We each have our own shack.

The shack is Young's metaphor for his hidden, wounded self. It is his real self—the self that hides behind the façade that projects his life as if it were a beautiful, well-kept house. The shack is Young's soul. It is something he and others built, just as our own shacks are built through our own experiences and choices, joys, and tragedies. William Paul Young, the author, is Mackenzie Allen Phillips, the main character in the story.

Young's soul is pictured in *The Shack* as a shack. The story is fictional but true. It is the story of a wounded soul filled with hidden secrets, addictions, and lies. In this story, Young's true self meets God.

Young has told his own personal story in several settings, most of them available by searching the Web.

He grew up as a missionary kid in New Guinea. Without cultural identity, physically and emotionally abused by his angry father, sexually abused by other children, he himself became a predator of sorts. To manage his wounds and medicate his pain, he became a religion addict—a perfectionistic performer. Ultimately, sexual sin overtook him in his late 30s while he served as a minister.

The years of guilt and shame took their toll on Paul. He built his own shack where the shame could reside, where wounds could hide. He attempted to win God's approval, just as he attempted to earn his own father's approval. He went to Bible College, then to seminary, and then into the ministry. He wanted a close relationship with God but did not know how to access it.

His life was filled with shame. On the outside, it looked like his house was in order, neatly kept as God's good minister. His perfectionistic attempts at performance hid the shame as he attempted to achieve some kind of self-worth. Maybe God would forgive him, love him, and accept him if he worked hard to compensate for the sin and shame he found himself unable to control. To do this, he had to stuff and numb his feelings. He did not know how to feel or talk about feelings. He was empty on the inside except for anger and shame, and he was mostly angry at himself.

He had built a shack hidden by a Hollywood front. The front was a lie—the godly preacher, leader; the shack was the truth—the sinner, the addict. But he could not speak the truth because it was too shameful. He could not speak the truth because that would risk everything. Shack-dwellers do not speak their truth because they fear rejection and shaming by others. If you really knew us, we shack-dwellers believe, you would not like us.

The Shack is Young's parable about how God met him at his shack and changed his life. God invited him to the shack. God met him in his pain and shame—not to judge it but to heal it; not to shame him but to love him. God does not invite us to the shack to shame us or express disappointment. God invites us to experience mercy and love, and God welcomes us in our own shacks in order to let us know how deeply loved we are.

The Shack invites us to enter into this metaphorical journey to the soul. Young writes with the prayer that perhaps through this story we will hear God's invitation to meet God at our own shacks and discover anew God's mercy.

The last paragraph of the acknowledgments in *The Shack* expresses this hope. Though originally written for his own children, as it was published to a wider audience, Young invested the novel with the specific purpose that readers might experience God's healing presence in their own shacks. It is his prayer, and it is mine as well.

CHAPTER 3

Your Shack, My Shack

What I feared has come upon me;
what I dreaded has happened to me.

We each have our own shacks.

Our shacks are partly constructed out of our childhood experiences. Missy's murderer, for example, was Paul Young himself, "twisted . . . into a terror" by his own father (163). Young's childhood in New Guinea gave him the eyes with which he sees the world. Our shacks are situated in the landscape of what we heard and experienced as children. Our "gut" has a default that was set by the time we were twelve years old.

Our "gut," our core belief about ourselves, determines our unconscious response to our experiences. We go there when we are stressed, threatened, or sad. We go there when we are afraid, and we cope with the world through the beliefs and behaviors that worked then. But what worked as children does not always work so well for adults. For example, overeating ("comfort food") may soothe an emotionally disturbed child for a moment, but it is a self-destructive behavior for an adult.

Our shacks are, in part, constructed out of life's tragic experiences. Young, for example, lost a brother and a niece to death, an experience that profoundly shaped the vibrancy of his life. Whether death, divorce, or addiction, among an almost limitless number of other tragedies, these experiences seep into our veins and sedate our joy. We can easily become lifeless zombies living out a meaningless existence because our shacks are so empty, dark, and depressing. We try to "make the best of it," but it often seems like a dead end. We medicate it with alcohol, drugs, sex, food, money, shopping, work, or whatever offers a moment of relief.

Our shacks are also self-made. We contribute material, labor, and time to their construction. Our own actions shape us, and sometimes they break us. Young's three-month affair broke him. Addictions, for example, arise out of the emotional holes dug throughout childhood and other life experiences, but they overwhelm us when we do not seek help. Sin may deceive us in our weakness, but when we pursue it, our shacks are decorated with our own pride, selfishness, and rebellion. While we may not have created our shack, we are responsible for its decor.

Shacks are where we hide our secrets—our sins, our resentments, our envies, our fears, our hurts, our sorrows, and our anger against God. These are the secrets we don't talk about.

We don't share them with others. We are afraid to share them. We fear what others would think of us if they knew our shacks.

We are afraid people will shame us when they hear our secrets. We've heard other people talk—the way they talk about celebrities when they know nothing about them. When we hear people use the secrets of others to condemn them and create an aura of self-righteousness, we fear they will do the same to us. It is better, we think, to remain silent. It is better, we suppose, to keep up our façade and bar everyone from our shacks.

We are afraid people will reject us when they hear our secrets. I vividly remember when my father confessed a grievous sin for which he was deeply penitent. Some of his close friends rejected him and no longer remained his intimates. I suspect they were never "intimates" in the first place—they did not know each other's shacks. When they discovered my father's shack through his self-disclosure, they discarded him and ostracized him.

We are afraid people will not hold our confidences when we tell them our secrets. Sharing our shacks is risky. It takes trust. But trust is what shacks lack most. That is one reason they are shacks rather than mansions. It is also a reason why faith is so difficult in the shack.

Most of all, I think, we are afraid of our own shacks. *We* know how dirty they are. We know their pain. We would much rather flee from our shacks—avoid them, ignore them, or pretend they don't exist. We don't want to go to our shacks and face ourselves. It is just too hard. It is easier to erect the Hollywood front and live an illusion. But we know it isn't real, and consequently, we hate ourselves because we know we are living a lie.

The shack is the last place where we want to meet God. He knows our shacks too well, and we are ashamed of them. We fear what God might do with us because of our shacks, and this fear is especially intense if we grew up with a kind of "hellfire and brimstone" God. At bottom, we don't trust God either.

I understand these feelings. I have experienced them in my shack. My shack, like yours, is complicated. It is filled—like most—with childhood experiences, life's tragedies, and my own sins. I will share some of them as we progress through this brief book, but it would probably be helpful to share a few pieces of my story—something of the condition of my shack—at this point.

My shack includes, among other things, death, divorce, and addiction.

I married Sheila when I was nineteen—already a graduate of college (part of my addiction to work my way toward approval)—but was widowed when I was twenty-two. Recovering from back surgery, which Sheila endured in order to carry a child full-term (we had already had one miscarriage), she died during her sleep when a blood clot passed through her heart and lungs. Her death was totally unexpected. I remember how embarrassed I was to grieve publicly. I remember how angry I was with God. I remember how lonely and empty I felt in the years following her death. I recognize now that I have truly grieved her death only in recent months.

I remarried, adopted Ashley, and welcomed Joshua and Rachel into this world. But early on it was apparent that Joshua had a problem. When he was six, we discovered he had a terminal genetic condition. Joshua died at the age of sixteen in 2001. My anger toward God returned, but I mostly tried to hide it.

Instead, I "chose" to play the "hero"—keeping my grief and tears private. I put "chose" in quotation marks, because in one sense, I did not choose it. It was my role in the world, so I thought. Consequently, I did not fully grieve Joshua's death either.

Then my marriage ended. Perhaps the grief was too much for us, but the hiddenness of my shack and the pretensions of my façade contributed greatly to the demise of my marriage. I was not emotionally present for my wife in our grief, because authentic presence would mean facing my shack, and I did not like to go there. It was too painful. In the brokenness of avoiding my shack, I contributed to the death of my own marriage and created more pain—not only for me, but for my wife, my children, and my family.

The shack became a breeding ground for addiction. I am a workaholic. I seek to fill my emptiness and avoid my pain by immersing myself in tasks or busyness. But it doesn't work. My shack is too big, too empty, and too tragic to be soothed by something as ultimately superficial as "success."

That is, in part, my shack. Facing my shack, entering it, and seeking God there has been my redemption. Perhaps you can see why—in some small way—Paul Young's *The Shack* became a meaningful story for me when I knocked on the door of my own shack.

Everyone has a shack. God is present in everyone's shack, waiting for us to show up. But shacks don't accommodate God very well—at least as we see our own shacks. In fact, we may have even been to the shack before (if only briefly) to seek God, but we could not find God; God was not there, so it seemed.

That, of course, is Mack's initial experience. And it is often our own as well.

CHAPTER 4

"God, I Hate You!"

Dear God.
I hate you.
Love,
MADELEINE (L'ENGLE)

I meditated on this brief prayer for months after I read it. Initially, I was horrified by how much I identified with the prayer, and I was troubled by the prayer's resonance in my soul. My first reaction, however, was "I get the point."

So did Mack. He had become furious with God over the years since Missy's death. But he went to the shack at God's invitation, doubting whether it really was God. As he entered the shack for the first time in over three years, his emotions exploded.

Mack bellowed the questions most sufferers ask, and most often they begin with the word "Why?" "Why did you let this happen? Why did you bring me here? Of all the places to meet you—why *here*?" In a blind rage, he threw a chair at the window and began smashing everything in sight with one of its legs. He vented his anger. His body released the emotions he had stored up in it.

Anger, if not resolved or healed, simmers inside of us. It becomes part of our body. We feel it in our chest, stomachs, shoulders, or neck. It destroys us from within. One day it will explode. For over three years, Mack had suppressed this anger, but now, alone in the shack, it poured out with a vengeance.

Fatigue ended his rampage but not his anger or despair. The pain remained; it was familiar to him, "almost like a friend." This darkness was Mack's closest friend, just as it was for Heman in Psalm 88:18. The "Great Sadness" burdened him and there was no escape (81). There was no one to whom he could turn, so he thought. Even God did not show up at the shack.

It would be better to be dead, to just get it over with, right? When great sadness descends on us, sometimes, like Mack, we think it is better to simply die and be rid of the pain. We think we would be better off dead if for no other reason than that the hurting would stop. Or, like Job, we might wish we had never been born (Job 3). Contemplating suicide, Mack cried himself to sleep on the floor of the shack.

Rising after what seemed like only a few minutes, Mack, still seething with anger and berating his own seeming idiocy, walked out of the shack. "I'm done, God" (82). He was worn out and finally gave up trying to reconnect with God in the midst of his pain.

This scene is Mack's true self. It is Mack in the shack. It is the pent-up, growing, and cancerous feelings of anger, bitterness, and resentment toward God. God, after all, did not protect Missy. God was no Papa to Missy in her deepest distress and need. The journey to discover God is not worth it. It is too hard, too gut-wrenching, and useless.

In his rage, Mack expressed the words that seethed underneath the anger, resentment, disappointment, and pain. "I hate you!" he shouted.

"I hate you." Them's fighting words, it seems to me. It expresses our fight (or, as in the case of Jacob, our wrestling) with God. Sometimes we flee our shacks, but at other times, we may go to our shacks to find God, only to discover we have a fight on our hands because God did not show up. This is Mack's initial experience.

The word "hate" stands for all the frustration, agitation, disgust, exasperation, and bewilderment we experience in the seeming absence of God as we live in a suffering, painful, and hurting world. "Hate" is a fightin' word—a representation of the inexplicable pain in our lives. The word is used as a weapon to inflict pain on the One whom we judge to be the source of our pain. Sometimes, perhaps, we are too polite with God. Sometimes we are not "real" with the Creator. Sometimes, like Jacob in Genesis 32, we need to wrestle with God.

I hear God's suffering servant Job in this word, though he never uses the specific term in his prayers. God has denied Job fairness and justice, and Job is bitter (Job 23:1; 27:2). God is silent. God "throws" Job "into the mud" and treats him as an enemy (30:19–20). God has attacked him, and death is Job's only prospect (30:21, 23). Job is thoroughly frustrated, bitter in his soul, and hopeless about his future (7:11, 21). He does not believe he will ever see happiness again (7:7). God was a friend who turned on him—"hate" might be an accurate description of Job's feelings as he sits on the dung heap.

And yet, just as in Madeleine's brief prayer, Job ends with "Love, Job." He speaks to God; Job is not silent. He does not turn from his commitment to God; he does not curse God or deny God. He seeks God. He laments, complains, wails, and angrily (even sarcastically) addresses the Creator. But he will not turn his back on God (23:10–12; 21:16).

The contrast between "I hate you" and "Love, Madeleine" is powerful. It bears witness to the tension within lament and our experience of the world's brokenness. Though deeply frustrated with the chaos surrounding us (whether it is divorce, the death of a son, the death of a wife, the plight of the poor, AIDS in Africa, terrorism, etc.) and with the sovereign God (Ps. 115:3; 135:6), we continue to sign our prayers (laments) with love. We have no one else to whom we can turn, and there is no one else worthy of our love or laments.

All of us can get to the point where we are done with God—that is, where we are done trying to "find God" in our shacks. The search for meaning, relationship, and love is often frustratingly slow and fruitless. "I hate you" may be the simplest and most shocking way to express our feelings about the whole mess.

Sometimes we blurt out language that expresses our feelings but does not line up with our faith. This can happen when our faith is shaken, confused, threatened, or slipping away. It is a common experience among believers when they go to their shacks.

We go to our shacks because we yearn for love, for relation-ship, for healing, or perhaps because we are desperate and there is nowhere else to go. We sign our prayers with love—"Love, Madeleine" or "Love, John Mark"—as an expression of hope. We want to love, to know love, and to experience love. It is out of this yearning we pray; it is out of this love we lament.

It is with love we say, "I hate you."

The poignant irony of that last sentence is, it seems to me, the essence of honest lament in a broken world.

CHAPTER 5

Getting a "Triune Shine"

*The LORD make his face shine upon you
and be gracious to you.*

"Triune Shine". . . what is that? Okay, I admit it is my own invention—at least, I could not find it anywhere when I googled it. But hear me out.

Many who have attended a 12-Step group for any length of time have heard about the "shine." It might be an "AA shine," or an SA, NA, OA, WA, and so on. The "shine" is the glow of recovery, and it stands in stark contrast with the first time someone attends a meeting. Addicts enter their first meeting despondent, shamed, and hopeless. They attend a meeting as a last gasp of sanity. Through recovery—working the steps that include confession and spiritual transformation—they begin to "shine" with hope, joy, and contentment.

I have turned the phrase on its head. When I say "Triune Shine," I do not mean that the Trinity has gone through recovery. I hope that is obvious. I mean the opposite. Rather, an encounter with the Triune God leaves a shine on our faces. It is the afterglow of meeting God in our shacks. It may not be an external glow, like when Moses left the Tent of Meeting after being with God, but it is the visible joy on faces once full of despair. The shine of Triune love lights up their faces.

Shine, of course, is what shacks need. Our shacks are broken, empty, dark, and hidden. They need healing, filling, light, and openness. When our true selves—our shacks—encounter the healing life and light of God in authentic loving relationship, we are transformed into beautiful images of God—beautiful homes or manicured log cabins. Shacks become mansions when we meet God in the circle of love. Our shacks get a Triune Shine.

This is what Mack experienced. Contemplating suicide, Mack cried himself to sleep on the floor of the shack. He was filled with anger, grief, and pain. This darkness was Mack's closest friend (much like Psalm 88:18); the "Great Sadness" was all too familiar to him.

Upon waking, Mack left the shack, only to turn around to see it transformed into a beautiful log cabin with a garden and gorgeous lake. Hearing laughter from the cabin, Mack cautiously approached its front door.

This is a critical moment in the parable, and it is a critical moment in our lives. Do we believe our shacks can become mansions? Do we believe our pain, hurt, and shame can be transformed into joy, beauty, and honor?

My own experience tells me it is well-nigh impossible to believe this in the midst of the pain itself. The pain is a fog that blinds us. Shame accuses us, and we feel the guilt and burden of our sin and addictions. I understand how impossible it is to believe; I've been there. The shack is hopeless; the fog is real; the soul is broken.

Addicts—and all who know themselves as sinners are addicts, since sin is itself an addiction—feel they deserve their shack. It is where they belong. They are unworthy of God's love. Many of us, shamed by our compulsions and powerless before them, do not believe we are good people. Surely, we think, God could not and does not love people like us.

Mack, standing on the front porch of the log cabin, is ready to knock on the door. Though enraged, he also feels like a screw-up. He does not know what to expect. What will he find behind the door of this cabin? He knows God invited him to the shack, but now the shack looks like a summer house. There is laughter inside, and he wonders how there can be laughter in a world where Missy is absent. This adds to his anger—how can anyone laugh in his shack, the place where Missy's blood still stains the floor?

I think the story, at this point, invites us to consider who our God is and how we envision God. When we knock on the door, who is this God who answers? When God opens the door to a shamed, guilt-ridden, hopeless but compulsively driven addict (sinner), how does God greet him? Will God berate us for our failures? Will God continue the shame by shaking a finger at us and railing at us? Will God's face confirm our sense that God is disappointed with us? Will God show disgust?

This is why I think this is a critical point in the parable. It says something about us and about who we believe God is. Will we knock? Will we seek God's face? And what will God do? How will God receive us? What do we expect?

Before Mack can even knock (just as Isaiah says, "before they call I will answer"—65:24), God—in the form of a gregarious African American woman—swings the door open and engulfs him in a loving bear-hug, lifting him off the ground and spinning him as if he were a young kid. God greets Mack with enthusiastic love.

No disappointment. No shaming. No hesitation. No rebuffing. No reminders of the past. No anger. No "I told you so." No "What were you thinking?" Instead, an exhilarating, loving, and enthusiastic expression of love.

When we encounter God, how will God receive us? Will God check the list of rights and wrongs? Will God evaluate us on a point system of some kind? Will God look over our record and shake His head with frustration and disappointment? I think not. Young's parable has it right.

Intellectually and theologically, I get it. I really do think God's reception of Mack is true. But, along with Mack, I find it emotionally difficult to receive it and believe it. It took Mack some time to adjust to this unexpected reception. He doubted his own joy at times, even as Papa spoke with him. I, too, still hesitate at times.

I grew up with an angry God for the most part; at least, I heard it that way. My God zapped Uzzah for touching the ark, killed Nadab and Abihu over something as small as where they got fire for the altar, and threw Adam and Eve out of the Garden over a piece of fruit. My simplistic hearing of those stories fired my fear of a God who was always looking for my mistakes and ready (even eager!) to give me what I deserve. God was, in my young imagination, Zeus, ready to fling thunderbolts at those who were displeasing.

I also grew up with a God whose approval I sought. At least I heard it that way. The little boy in me saw God as the One to please in order to gain approval. I performed to please this God; I sought applause and delight. If I could do enough, then God would be pleased with me. If I did it right, God would applaud me. It was a kind of religious perfectionism. Add that to workaholism and you have one tired dude running all over the world looking for Papa's approval. That was (is?) me.

Young's parable offers a different picture—a God who deeply loves us and is delighted to be with us. I already knew it intellectually, but emotionally, I needed to feel it in my gut. I need to know—to know in ways beyond mere cognition, reaching deep within my soul, my shack—that God delights in me and yearns to give me a big ole bear-hug. I need to know God deeply loves me even when my performance is not "good enough." I need to feel deep down within me that God already delights in me, and I don't need to seek divine approval. Young's thrilling picture of Mack's encounter with God provides an image—a relational picture—I can hang my emotional hat on.

Even more . . . God is already present in my shack, waiting for me to show up, waiting for me to become my true self. When I come to my shack, and when you go to yours, God is already there. God is waiting to renew, sustain, enjoy, and pursue relationship with us. We find ourselves, even in the shack, right where we were designed to be—in the center of God's circle of relational, Triune love.

Ultimately, Mack leaves the shack with a "Triune Shine." He comes to know all his "best treasures are now hidden in" the Triune God rather than in his little tin box with Missy's picture (238). His encounter with the Triune God has filled his emptiness, and his dark, horrifying nightmares have now become colorful, vibrant dreams.

The "Triune Shine" is what I call that deep recognition that I am loved by the Father, filled with the Spirit, and live in the life of the Son. The "Triune Shine" is the joy of living in a circle of relationship with Papa, Jesus, and Sarayu.

When we recognize the powerlessness of our shacks (we can't fix them ourselves), accept that God is already present in our shacks to restore us to sanity, and we choose to embrace that relationship by surrendering to that love, our shacks become log cabins (maybe even mansions).

Twelve-steppers will recognize that last paragraph as their first three steps into spiritual recovery—I am powerless, there is a higher power, and I have decided to surrender. It is a long journey; it is not a quick fix. But it is a divine promise.

CHAPTER 6

Living in a Colorless World

Even the darkness will not be dark to you;
the night will shine like the day,
for darkness is as light to you.

PSALM 139:12

The first time I encountered the phrase The "Great Sadness" in *The Shack*, it immediately resonated with me. I knew exactly what my own Great Sadness was, though I did not as yet know what Mack's was or what Young's own personal sadness was.

My Great Sadness, like Mack's, colored everything in my life. It touched every aspect of my being—the way I looked at the world, the way I experienced life. It sapped the color out of life and turned everything to a dingy gray and, at times, an "inky darkness," as *The Shack* describes so well. The Great Sadness tints our vision with shades of gray and darkness

51

rather than with bright, vibrant, and life-affirming colors (198). It makes us see the world through tinted windows. It is like living life with sunglasses permanently attached to our eyes. It is worse than blinding; it distorts the goodness of God.

Mack's Great Sadness is his missing, and presumed dead, daughter Missy. For Paul Young, the author, Missy is a metaphor for his murdered childhood innocence; it is his wounded child. His Great Sadness is lost innocence and unhealed childhood wounds.

My own Great Sadness is the cumulative experience of the deaths of my wife, son, and second marriage. To many, I have given the appearance of strength and joy. But I now realize that was mostly a façade. It was an unintentional deception. I had built a Hollywood front around my Great Sadness. It is easier to put up a veneer than to deal with the real hurt and pain that goes so deep you can't imagine ever being rid of it. It is easier to deceive yourself into thinking grief has been resolved than to actually live through it.

The Great Sadness shapes how life is lived. It becomes our closest friend; it is darkness (Ps. 88:18). I hid that darkness deep within me, giving no one—not even my wife—access to the hurt. It hurt too much to speak it. In addition, to acknowledge the pain would shatter my heroic self-image, my assumed identity. But instead of heroism, the Great Sadness had become, as for Mack, my identity as I lost joy in my inner soul and propped up the image of a superman, the great comforter.

While I have no doubt that God worked through me in ways beyond my imagination to help others, I now know that I did not deal with my own grief in healthy ways. It seemed easier to ignore, numb, or escape the feelings of grief than to live through them. Mack's journey, paralleling my own in many ways, is the story of dealing with grief and anger in ways that erected a barrier between God and himself as well as between himself and others. The Great Sadness prevented intimacy.

My Great Sadness stalled my spiritual growth; honestly, it more than stalled it. It radically diminished it. And, in February 2008, I crashed emotionally. I, like Mack, was trapped by an emotionless, silent grief and anger. It was an anger toward God as well as myself, perhaps mostly at myself. I was not living up to my own self-image; I was not honest with my own pain. Instead of seeking spiritual nourishment, I performed. I thought that would do it. I thought excelling would heal the grief, soothe the anger, and get God and me on the same page. But my performance was an escape; it was a religious addiction, it was workaholism. I was running from my grief rather than living through it.

I was, in fact, holding back the tears; I was ashamed of tears. *The Shack* renewed my appreciation for tears. The waterfall near the shack is a symbol for tears. Tears can "drain away" the pain and replace it with relief (175); they are God's gift to cry "out all the darkness" (228). The Holy Spirit collects tears, and they become part of God's own heart. Indeed, the Father weeps with us and sheds tears. God, as Young rightly pictures it, is able to absorb our pain into God's own life. That is the empathetic, redemptive, atoning love of God.

My first experience with Great Sadness was Sheila's death. I was devastated. Our dreams, hopes, and plans for the future were gone in a single moment. It was a sudden tear in my universe that left me, seemingly, nothing. The future would be totally unlike the past; the future would be totally different than what we had planned and what I had anticipated.

Since February 2008, I have focused my personal and spiritual energy on living through my past grief traumas—to relive them in order to better integrate them into my psyche, my soul, and reset my response to those events. A vivid memory that symbolizes my trauma is the conclusion of Sheila's funeral. After a lengthy visitation period and funeral, I was practically carried out of the church building on the shoulders of my family. As we walked out the front door of the building, the whole town of Ellijay, Georgia, it seemed, were there watching, including the choir of Potter Christian School from Bowling Green, Kentucky. I felt utterly embarrassed. Everyone saw my grief; everyone saw my "weakness." I felt exposed, vulnerable. This has had a profound effect on my subsequent grief—more than I would really care to admit.

I don't know how many share that sense of embarrassment with me, or if I am the only one, but it was real for me. My embarrassment at grieving so deeply, so openly, and so despondently was perhaps rooted in my lack of experience with grief. Perhaps my church's lack of modeling grief is to blame, perhaps my own personality, perhaps my inexperience with biblical laments, perhaps the cultural image of "big boys don't cry," perhaps my faulty theology of hope ("she is in a better place, so don't cry"), perhaps a false sense of what male strength looks like coupled with my father's own seeming emotional distance—well, there are many, many reasons, and perhaps all of them have an element of truth.

I know, however, that experience has shaped me in unconscious ways. It has prevented, to some degree, deep grieving in other losses—at least public grief. I have avoided grief rather than fully embracing it. Despite my intellectual knowledge of grief, lament, and tears, I did not let myself fully grieve. I did not let myself cry. I wanted to avoid the embarrassment as well as the pain. I did not want to live through that grief again; I did not want to feel it, since I knew how awful it was.

I am grateful that in recent years the church has increasingly acknowledged the function, role, and need of communal lament. As lament is taught, modeled, and experienced, the kind of embarrassment I felt on May 2, 1980, is less likely, and the opportunities to fully experience grief are enlarged. When the community laments, we grievers do not feel so alone.

I am handling that embarrassment better now—partly because I am grieving, partly because I have immersed myself in the biblical laments in the past ten years, partly because I have sat with others in their grief, partly because I also see the love with which that community surrounded me at that funeral—but it is an image that lingers in my mind in subtle ways. I think embarrassment is part of my past now rather than my present, but it has shaped me and is part of the material of my shack.

Psalm 6, though primarily about physical healing, is a text I read through the lens of psychological and emotional healing. I hear myself in that prayer; I hear the yearnings of my own heart. I am sick at heart, the psalmist sings, "I am worn out from sobbing. All night I flood my bed with weeping, drenching it with my tears." Those tears, however, are a defense. They send evil away because "the LORD has heard my weeping" (Ps. 6:3a, 6, 8b).

Tears are wonderful healers; they are divine gifts. Tears release emotional stress. Biochemically, tears of grief release

CHAPTER 7

Stuck in the Great Sadness

My spirit is broken . . .
My eyes have grown dim with grief;
my whole frame is but a shadow.

JOB 17:1A, 7

The Great Sadness wore on Mack like a heavy quilt. He felt it in his chest as it squeezed the joy out of life. It was so present that the sadness was present in practically every conversation between Nan and Mack. The sadness so permeated Mack's heart that, even as he cooked with Papa and walked with Jesus, it was still with him.

Mack was stuck in the sadness, and he could not shake it. It would not relent.

One of the more significant points *The Shack* raises is what fuels the Great Sadness when we are stuck in it. Why does it continue? Why does it sink in deeper? Why does it become an identity rather than an experience endured? These questions are pursued in one of the more outstanding chapters in *The Shack*, "Here Come Da Judge."

Mack encounters Sophia, the Wisdom of God. Just as in Proverbs 8, God's wisdom is personified as a woman. Sophia invites Mack to sit in the judge's chair. Mack will decide how to run the world. The dialogue is analogous to Job's encounter with God in Job 38–42, and presumably Young wants us to draw the link. As God questioned Job, so Sophia questions Mack. Though Mack sits as judge—because this is what he has presumed himself to be in his anger—Sophia questions him about love, blame, and punishment.

The dialogue reveals the underlying problem. Sadness is never supposed to be an "identity." When the Great Sadness becomes our identity rather than just part of our experience, we get stuck in the Sadness instead of living through it. It becomes our identity because it consumes our experience, becomes the sum total of our experience, and colors everything we are, believe, know, and hope. It affects the way we love and our ability to love.

Then the question comes. Sophia asks what "fuels" the Sadness. She answers her own question with a rhetorical one, "That God cannot be trusted?" (163). Rather than trust God, Mack blamed God. This is the critical juncture; this is the orienting choice humans make. This is how we get stuck.

We do not trust—at a deeply emotional level—that God really is good. We do not trust—with our hearts as much as our heads—that God really loves us. We do not trust—with our gut—that God has a purpose for the world, for our own children, and for us. We doubt that every story participates in God's Grand Purpose, and we doubt that God's interest in everyone's story (even Missy's or Joshua's) is good, loving, and meaningful.

This lack of trust prevents us from fully living in the present because we regret our past or fear our future. As we wait for the next shoe to drop or live with the guilt of the past, we cannot immerse ourselves in the joy of the present. Like many, including the fictional Mack and the real Paul Young, I have lived much of my life in the past or the future rather than the present. When we live in the past or future, we live in fear rather than trust. I am only now learning to live in the present, to live one day at a time.

I have learned that Jesus is right. It is rather annoying to finally learn something you should have figured out long ago. My head seemed to always escape into the future—planning what I would say, what I would do, what I would write, and how I would play the hero. The day was not sufficient to itself—I had to live in the future to avoid the present pain. I avoided the pain by investing my energies in the future rather than living through the evil (pain) of the day. Jesus's caution is now more real to me than it had been in the past. "Each day has enough trouble of its own" (Matt. 6:34).

"One day at a time" is my new mantra. Oh, I've known it, spoken it, advised it, but rarely lived it. And I don't think I have ever known exactly what it meant in practical terms, at least in my own life. I'm only beginning to understand and live it now.

Jesus calls us to live in the present—to experience the present without worry or fear of the future. The present is all I really have, and if I want to look life in the eye, I must live life today. I must live in the now. To live one day at a time is to pray for and receive our "daily" bread without living in our tomorrows with anxiety. To avoid grief—to avoid the present experience of grief—is to circumvent God's healing process by escaping it, numbing it, or attempting to transcend it by some kind of heroism or avoidance mechanism rather than living through the pain.

Living in the past or future is largely driven by fear—fear of past secrets, hurts, and pains, or future ones. As Jesus tells Mack, whenever he imagined the future, it was filled with fear because that imagination never included God's own presence in the future. The future without God is indeed bleak. No wonder fear dominates when we live in the future.

Fear drives our imaginations. We run through all the scenarios, plan our responses, and still live with the fear that everything may go wrong. As much as we try to control our lives in order to minimize fear, we are still afraid. Why? "Because you don't believe," Jesus said to Mack. Whenever fears dominate, they drive out love, and there is little love because there is little faith. At root, because fear is so deeply embedded in the heart, "you neither believe I am good nor know deep in your heart that I love you" (144).

Exactly! We trust neither God's goodness nor God's love. This was not a new idea for me: I have said it before (in my earlier book *Yet Will I Trust Him*), and I have known it in my head, but this truth failed to sink deeply into my heart, into my emotional being, into my gut. The baggage of my life, for the most part, prevented God's love from fully saturating my soul.

This, for me, has been the value of *The Shack*. It has given me powerful emotional imagery to explore my grief, recognize my own "shack," embrace the reality of God's love at a new level, and see beyond the Sadness. God has used this story to connect me more fully, more deeply with God's Story.

Embracing the distinction between the Great Sadness as our identity and the Great Sadness as an experience through which we live is important for getting "unstuck." Living one day at a time allows us to experience the sadness without getting stuck in it, because it alleviates our fear of the future. But learning to trust is the positive action that prevents identifying the sadness with our core.

Papa feels the sadness too. Papa weeps. Jesus weeps, and Sarayu collects tears. But this does not become their identity. Rather, love is their identity. Because they love, they feel the sadness, but the sadness does not supplant love as the core experience of the Father, Son, and Spirit. They are love.

In the telescoped telling of this parable, the burden of Mack's Great Sadness is lifted. Mack no longer considers it part of his identity. What happened? Mack came to believe— to truly trust—that, despite his tragic experiences, God really does love him and Missy.

When we learn to trust that God really loves us—when we know we are beloved, we can feel the sadness without it becoming our identity. Love is our identity, not the Great Sadness. God is love, and we are created in the image of God.

For years when I thought of Sheila's funeral, I could only see the embarrassment, tears, grief, and pain. The fog of the Great Sadness colored everything gray. I could not see the love present there. I could not see the love of the children from Potter Children's Home who came to sing at the funeral; I could not see the love of my parents and siblings; I could not see the love the Pettit family (my in-laws) had for me, as if I were their own son (and to this day they still call me "son" or "brother"); I could not see the love of my best man, who came at great expense from Oklahoma to stand beside me at the grave (thanks, Bruce!); I could not see—the list could go on and on.

The Great Sadness distorts the goodness and love of God. It blinds us to love. The fog creates distrust and fear. But the love of God is nevertheless present in the Great Sadness. God was with Missy. God is present in our shacks. God was present at Sheila's funeral. God wept with me.

Surrounded by love, God spoke a word into my heart that day that I can only now begin to hear: "You are my beloved."

CHAPTER 8

Gardening with God

*The LORD will guide you always,
he will satisfy your need . . .
You will be like a well-watered garden,
like a spring whose waters never fail.*

ISAIAH 58:11

A garden rests beside The Shack in Mack's vision, and it represents Mack's own heart, his soul. It is a chaotic mess but beautiful, and, more importantly, tended by the Holy Spirit. Indeed, speaking for the Triune community, the Spirit assures Mack that it is also *"our* garden." There is hope for the mess in which our gardens find themselves, because God works in this garden; it is God's garden too! Our gardens are messes but also beautiful as they are filled with meaning, significance, and purpose.

Young paints a picture of Sarayu and Mack gardening together. They are pulling up weeds and tending the garden. The Spirit, doing the lion's share of the work, cooperates with Mack in beautifying the garden. Together they prepare ground for a new planting. They dig up the roots that will impede what they will plant. Mack will soon plant new life in the ground with the help of the Triune God.

Amidst the "chaos in color" (130), however, there is a "wound in the garden" (133). It is Mack's pain, his Great Sadness. This is the area that the Spirit and Mack worked to prepare for fresh plantings, for healing.

Young offers a wonderful picture of the somatic (using the physical body) and psychodramatic endurance of grief. Papa leads Mack to the body of his daughter; Mack weeps for her and carries her back to the garden for burial. Mack buries her in his heart—in the ground prepared by the Spirit, with a casket made by the carpenter Jesus, and in the loving embrace of the Father. It is a pure act of love. With their presence, the garden blossoms with the beauty of Missy's life and God's heart.

Mack's encounter with the Triune God gave him perspective. He sees his life as a garden tended by God. Through his storytelling and his own recovery, Young is able to assume once again the innocent trust of a child in the presence of God.

The power of psychodrama is this: it brings body and soul into relation with unresolved trauma or grief. It is not merely cognitive (thinking), but it is somatic (done with your body) and communal (done with other people). When there is unresolved trauma in our unconscious, we revert back to that trauma when we are triggered by an analogous experience. We then react to the present trigger as if we are again experiencing the original trauma. Consequently, we tend to intensify feelings inappropriate to the situation or transfer feelings from the past event to the present. The present does not necessarily warrant those feelings, and this confuses people in relationship with us. Grievers, then, tend to withdraw emotionally in order to protect themselves from those horrendous feelings.

On November 14, 2007, my good friend and colleague at Lipscomb University, Mike Matheny, died after a three-year struggle with a brain tumor. Mike—both of us are fifty at the time—is a dear friend. We talk often about our great loves—the Psalms and baseball. He is (even now!) a Yankee fan; I am a Cubs fan. But both of us are fans of the lament Psalms. Both of us prayed those laments and taught Psalms at Lipscomb. I miss him terribly, but I imagine that even now he sings with the saints around the throne of God in both praise ("worthy is the Lamb," Revelation 5) and lament ("how long, O Lord?", Revelation 6).

Mike's death was a traumatic trigger for me. The last time I visited Mike, it was as if I were with my son, Joshua, in his last days. Both Mike and Joshua were in hospice, incapacitated and nonverbal. My time with Mike was a psychological reversion to the trauma of Joshua's death, which was then a reversion to Sheila's death. It was as if I were at Joshua's bedside as well as Mike's, as if I were again being carried out of Sheila's funeral. My gut took me there, because those grief traumas were yet unresolved.

In the wake of that reversion, I shut down emotionally. Even my funeral sermon at Mike's service was devoid of emotion. I did not want to feel that pain. It was a pain I was all too familiar with—it was my Great Sadness, and my way of dealing with it was to withdraw and numb my feelings. Not feeling the pain was, it seemed to me, better than feeling the pain. I did not realize what I was doing to myself.

I thought I had resolved my grief, and even believed I was relatively healthy, but I was actually deceiving myself. I was playing the hero again. A hero, of course, cannot let himself be embarrassed by tears or uncontrolled grief. He must hide it with laughter and avoid intense conversations about it.

The hero must be strong and model how to handle life's tragedies. But I am no hero. On the contrary, instead of living through my grief, I avoided it. I tried to jump over my grief and leap—like superman—over tall buildings in a single bound.

I am now grateful my leap was actually a crash, and the crash has become a moment of divine grace, a divine awakening. Hitting the wall of unresolved trauma has given me the opportunity to truly experience my grief—to revisit, relive, and reconstruct the meaning of my grief, to re-enter the world of lament and truly feel what has become a journey of authentic healing. And for this I am grateful to God and grateful for the people God put into my life. They have supported me, showed me grace, and modeled redemptive love.

Psychodrama, in my experience, provided a way to re-experience the past trauma in a safe environment in order to reconfigure its meaning. Psychodrama confronts the past in a concrete somatic (bodily) and spiritual experience so that we symbolically but nevertheless authentically relive the past trauma. This confrontation undermines attempts to flee (escape) from the trauma, to fight the trauma with intensified feelings, or to freeze (numb) our feelings. While those strategies protect us in the initial moments of grief, if we get stuck in any one of them, then the unresolved trauma will negatively affect our sense of peace and our relationships with others.

Psychodrama resolves trauma by reorganizing a memory. By entering the past trauma through role play, one is able to gain perspective and assign new meaning to the experience. It is another way of bringing emotional "closure" to an experience. The drama creates a new narrative—it is a redoing of the past through undoing the past. It gives us a chance for a "do over." The new narrative provides a new frame of reference for drawing meaning from the event as we reconstruct the past with new awareness, perspective, and insight.

Through one psychodrama, I re-experienced the grief of Sheila's funeral. It opened again for me the floodgates of tears, which I had unconsciously held in reserve through numbing and withdrawal. Through another, I recreated Joshua's funeral with a few friends in my home. Once again the tears flowed in the security of the loving care of my friends.

When Papa led Mack to Missy's body and Mack carried her body back to the garden for burial, this was a psychodramatic act which allowed Mack to retell the story of Missy's death. This time, it was framed by Triune love, empathy, and care. This time, it was experienced in the daylight of the garden rather than in the darkness of the Great Sadness. There were still tears—it was still sad—but the tears were shared and then wiped by a divine Presence that Mack trusted and loved.

Mack was no longer "stuck" in his Great Sadness.

CHAPTER 9

The Eyes of Jesus

The Lord turned around and looked straight at Peter.

LUKE 22:61

One of the most vivid scenes in the Gospel of Luke is Peter's three denials, particularly "the look."

The verbs are intensive, descriptive, and full of significance. "Turned around" involved twisting or reversing; it is turning 180 degrees. Jesus turned around—he "converted," as the term is sometimes translated—to look at Peter. But it was no mere glance; it was an intense gaze. Jesus looked at Peter with piercing, discerning eyes.

> *Turning his body toward Peter, the Lord's eyes rested on Peter.* [JMH amplified]

The next verbs in Luke 22:61–62 describe Peter's response. He "remembered" what Jesus had predicted, and "he went and wept bitterly." Confronted with his betrayal, Peter remembered. He then escaped; he ran away. And then he wailed violently—a visible, audible, wrenching sob. Peter, faced with his denial and memory, was a totally broken person. Remembering Jesus's prediction—and, no doubt, his own insistence that it would never happen—he burst into tears.

What did Peter see in the eyes of Jesus that pierced his heart? What did those eyes tell him?

What did Mack expect to see behind the door of his shack? What kind of God did he expect to meet? Would God look at him angrily? Accusingly? Contemptibly? Or would those eyes express love, peace, and forgiveness?

What did Peter see in the eyes of Jesus?

I think that how we answer this question will probably say more about our own vision of God than it would about Peter's. We can't get inside of Peter's head, but we can examine our own. Our root image of God—perhaps one we learned in childhood, one that is at the core of our inner being—will probably shape how we feel this text.

We can easily imagine what Peter felt. No doubt he felt shame and guilt. We have all felt the same when confronted with our sins or our angry outbursts. That shame and guilt taps into something deep within us, and our core understanding of God will shape how we deal with it.

For some, the eyes of Jesus may be primarily condemning. Peter sinned; he did not measure up. He did not keep the law; he betrayed a friend. The law condemns him, and Jesus condemns him. At the root of this perception is an angry God, a judge who strictly administers the law without mercy. Jesus, with these eyes, is insulted and offended. "How dare Peter deny me! I thought he was my friend! Didn't he say he would go to death with me! He deserves whatever he gets!"

As we noted earlier, this God is the Zeus who sits on the throne, ready to fling lightning bolts at those who deserve his vengeance. These eyes convey no hope, no redemption. Unfortunately, they are the eyes many have lived with for years, even when intellectually they know the story of grace much better than their gut will let them feel. It is what some got from their parents—a series of spankings, condemnations. They heard the message that they were bad kids and deserved punishment. Or they have met those eyes in the faces of church people—yes, Christians. Are these the eyes that met Peter's eyes?

For others, the eyes of Jesus may be primarily filled with disappointment. Peter disappointed Jesus; he had hoped for better. Peter knew better; he knew he should not deny his Lord, but he did nevertheless. Peter had expectations of himself. Even if everyone else ran away, he would not. He would die with Jesus if necessary. The disappointed eyes are the opposite of what Peter wanted. He wanted approval, praise, and honor. To feel Jesus's disappointment meant he was seeking Jesus's commendation.

Commendation is what we often seek from parents as children; we don't want to disappoint our parents. Some parents, when disappointed, shame their children. "I knew you couldn't do it. Why can't you be like Johnny? When will you ever learn? Do I have to do everything myself? I can't trust you with anything. I'll have to finish what you started." We tend to project this onto God, who then becomes like the shaming parent voicing disapproval, disappointment, and dissatisfaction. Are these the eyes that met Peter's eyes?

At my core, my childhood images—images I learned, but surely few people, if any, ever intentionally taught me—tend to see the eyes of an angry, disappointed God. My sin gave me a toxic shame that meant I was worthless, a mistake, a screw-up (like Mack felt). I needed to get God's approval, to get on God's good side. I wanted God to like me and certainly not punish me. So, I needed to work harder, better, faster . . . to do more, to do enough.

Intellectually, I know that last paragraph is bogus. Emotionally, however, it has been a different story. And so when I worked my way to a hellacious screw-up—working for what I thought God wanted but actually working myself to death, even a spiritual death—I immediately felt God's disappointment. "John Mark, you should've known better." Or "John Mark, how could you?!" Or "John Mark, what were you thinking?"

But what did Peter see in the eyes of Jesus?

I don't think he saw condemning, judgmental eyes. Neither do I think he saw disappointed eyes. I think he saw sadness, a compassionate and hopeful sadness. Jesus grieved for Peter. His eyes expressed sympathy and caring. They were redemptive eyes. Jesus is more interested in relationship with Peter than in excluding, punishing, or shaming him. Jesus is the divine loving brother who grieves over the failures and hurts of his siblings but does not give up on them. Peter saw in Jesus's eyes his ongoing compassionate, forgiving, loving prayer that Peter would be strengthened by this experience, and the hope in his eyes assured Peter that he would.

In our betrayals, our sins, our denials, what do we see in the eyes of Jesus? With Peter we will remember and weep bitterly. That is understandable and healthy. But also with Peter may we gain strength through the compassionate redemptive hope in Jesus's eyes.

Mack asked Papa: "Honestly, don't you enjoy punishing those who disappoint you?" Papa "turned toward Mack" and, with "deep sadness in her eyes," said: "I am not who you think I am, Mackenzie." God weeps over our sin because God knows what sin does to us. When we sin, we enter into a self-destruct mode. God is not disappointed. Instead, God weeps and turns that mourning into joy when he heals our wounds (121–122).

I think Paul Young got that right. Intellectually, I understand it. Emotionally, well, I'm still learning.

Jesus's eyes, though sad, anticipated the joy of redemption for Peter, for me, for all of us.

CHAPTER 10

Forgiving Others

Be kind and compassionate to one another,
forgiving each other,
just as in Christ God forgave you.

EPHESIANS 4:32

Forgiveness is just beneath the surface in the first half of Young's parable. By the end, it becomes central to Mack's healing. Our shacks only become mansions through the grace of forgiveness. Without forgiveness—both receiving and giving—our shacks will remain broken. Without forgiveness—both receiving and giving—we are "stuck" in the Great Sadness.

Mack thought he had come to the end of his spiritual journey at the moment he finally learned to trust Papa. Trust develops when we learn to enjoy the circle of God's Triune loving relationship. Mack had arrived, or so he thought.

Papa took Mack on a "healing trail," but it was not just about Missy's body. It was about something much deeper and much more difficult. If Mack is going to fully experience the circle of divine love, then he must also enter into the inner circle of forgiveness. Papa says, "I want to take away one more thing that darkens your heart." Mack must actually forgive the one who murdered Missy, the one he had earlier condemned to hell.

I believe this is one of the most stirring sections of *The Shack,* one filled with profound wisdom as well as striking statements. How do people forgive the one who murdered their child?

Giving forgiveness is exactly that—it is an act of grace, a gift. Forgiveness is not owed; it is not a debt we must pay. Forgiveness cannot be demanded, coerced, or even expected by offenders. Forgiveness is given.

At one level, forgiving is therapeutic and healthy. It does something for us and inside of us, including lowering blood pressure and decreasing heart rates. It releases negativity; it vents the poison that corrupts our souls. It is freedom from repressed negative emotions. When we refuse to forgive, we fuel a cancer that devours us. Consequently, forgiveness is something we do for ourselves. We forgive for the sake of our own mental and physical health.

But forgiveness is much more than a humanistic act of self-transformation. Forgiveness participates in the divine life. It is being with others in the way God is with us. We love as God loves. When we forgive, we participate in God's redemptive movement within the world; we participate in God's own forgiving act. And we come to know God's love as an insider through forgiving others.

Viewed in this way, forgiveness arises out of the work of God's Spirit in our hearts. It arises out of our own experience of having received forgiveness from God, the empowerment of the Spirit to forgive as God forgives, and the sense of security and assurance that we are beloved by God no matter how others may treat us or what they think of us.

Remembering our own mistakes and sins empowers forgiveness. If God has forgiven us, then who are we to withhold forgiveness from others? Are we better than they? And, ah, that might be the very problem that hinders us . . . our pride, our sense of superiority, our self-righteousness.

What hinders forgiveness is our own resentment and bitterness. We humans tend to wallow in self-pity, blame everyone else for how we feel, and fail to act positively with our negative feelings. This resentment and bitterness leads to negative actions such as revenge, so that we return evil for evil instead of forgiving the evil done against us.

Yet, there remains in us a deep yearning for justice, even revenge. As Mack says, even when justice is not available, we still want revenge as the next best thing. We think it will satisfy our deepest yearnings about evil. Papa's response is brilliantly on point, "Mack, for you to forgive this man is for you to release him to me and allow me to redeem him" (226). Mack and the reader are reminded of an earlier scene where Sophia gloried in how love grounded the triumph of mercy at the cross rather than giving everyone justice.

God wants to redeem even those who have wounded us, and he prefers mercy for them just as he prefers it for us. Our act of forgiveness releases them to God and takes the burden off us. We can let go of resentment, bitterness, and vengeance when we leave it in God's hands. Instead of taking matters into our own hands or grabbing the offender by the throat with threats, we let go. We let go and let God handle it.

Anger becomes ungodly when it turns to revenge. When we return evil for evil, then we become an abuser rather than the abused. When we take vengeance into our own hands, then we become judge, jury, and executioner. We become God.

Are we still angry about the wounds? Yes! Anger, at least in some form, is certainly a healthy response toward abuse. When things go wrong, as Papa notes, anger is both a natural and appropriate response. "But," he continues, "don't let the anger" hinder forgiveness and the removal of "your hands from around his neck" (229). Forgiving someone does not excuse their actions, but it does release them from our judgment and places them in the hands of God, who will handle justice in the world. Forgiveness means we are no longer vindictive, seeking to do the other harm. We no longer take them by the throat but hand them over to God.

Yet, when we have experienced hurt through the offense of another, anger is a natural and healthy response. There is nothing ungodly about a rape victim's anger toward their assailant. There is nothing ungodly about an abused wife's anger toward her husband. There is nothing ungodly about anger toward one's sexual abuser. Part of the process of forgiveness may, in fact, involve confronting the other person with what they have done. Forgiveness does not mean that what the other person did is okay, but it does give the forgiver space to be okay about their past.

Forgiveness doesn't seem fair, does it? That is the joy in receiving it, and the difficulty in giving it. None of us wants fairness when we are receiving forgiveness. Instead, we tend to want our "pound of flesh" before giving it. In forgiving, we not only release the offender to the judgment of God; we also release ourselves from the weight of resentment, which is too heavy to bear and will only sour the sweetness in our lives. Resentment is a poison we ingest while expecting the other person to die. It only harms the one who harbors the resentment.

Actually, resentment and bitterness arise from our own wounds, out of our Great Sadness. Life has wounded all of us—we have been betrayed, neglected, and attacked by others, and even (as it may seem) by God. As a result, we want to protect ourselves, rely on our own self-sufficiency, and blame everyone else rather than take responsibility for our lives. Thus we resent others when they hurt us. We resent rather than forgive, because this is how we think others have treated us. Our negative self-image, developed through childhood and other life experiences, yields a negative reaction to hurt in the form of resentment. Unchecked, this resentment leads to revenge.

How do we let go of resentment? Here is an ancient practice that may help—it is one Papa suggested to Mack. To forgive and let go, pray for the offender every day for a month. Every day say to God, "I forgive 'Joe,' and I want you to give him every blessing that I seek in my own life." This habit—which is also suggested in the Alcoholics Anonymous "Big Book"—is liberating and enriching. Whenever I feel resentment, I pray for those I resent, and I pray daily for them until I feel the release—and it may take weeks—or months!

This does not mean that the forgiver must now reconcile with the forgiven. Forgiveness is not reconciliation. Forgiveness—as an act of grace toward another—can happen without reconciliation, since the other may not receive the forgiveness, may not think they need forgiveness, or may not want to renew (or begin) the relationship. It only takes one to forgive, but it takes two to reconcile. While forgiveness may pave the way for reconciliation, forgiveness does not necessarily lead to reconciliation, and reconciliation is not required for forgiveness.

Reconciliation takes much longer than forgiveness since reconciliation involves a cooperative process of mutual understanding. That takes time, intimacy, and trust. Reconciliation assumes rebuilt trust, and that is a painful, time-consuming process. Reconciliation may never come—some people never reconcile with God, for example. But reconciliation is not necessary for forgiveness.

The "miracle" of reconciliation, however, begins with the "miracle" of forgiveness. There can be no reconciliation except where the offended forgives the offender. I think the word "miracle" is appropriate, because such acts are divinely enabled and are themselves participation in the divine life. We will, according to Papa, discover in our own hearts what allows us to build a path of reconciliation between the parties involved. The miracle begins with God working in our hearts and not waiting for the "other person" to make the first move. The first move is forgiveness; it was God's own first move, right? Christians know it as the Cross.

Forgiveness does not mean the offense was insignificant, or that it did not hurt, or that there was no reason for anger.

Rather, forgiveness is our decision to let God handle the justice, to let go of the other person's throat, to let go of the resentment, and to let go of any personal desire to punish. Positively, and more significantly, forgiveness means desiring for that person what you desire for yourself and treating that person the way God treats you. In short, it is to love them, even if they—in their minds—are our enemies.

We can only love when we feel loved by God. Our acceptance of God's own forgiveness and our experience of the divine circle of love surrounds us with safety and security. We forgive out of that secure place—the place where we hear God say, "You are my beloved no matter what your past; you are loved." That love overflows into forgiveness for others.

At bottom, "to forgive is divine" (Alexander Pope).

CHAPTER 11

Forgiving Ourselves

This then is how we know that we belong to the truth,
and how we set our hearts at rest in his presence
whenever our hearts condemn us. For God is greater
than our hearts, and he knows everything.

1 JOHN 3:19–20

Mack has a problem with himself as well as with the murderer. He lives under the burden of self-blame and self-punishment, even self-hatred. He deserves, so he thinks, to live in the Great Sadness because he did not protect his daughter.

The Great Sadness, when we feel responsible in some way (no matter how small!), creates a self-perpetuating cycle of blame and punishment. It becomes a form of self-flagellation. We deserve the pain, so we think. How can Mack enjoy life when Missy is dead? He has no right to joy and peace. He did not protect her. Sometimes he even feels like God is punishing him because of how he treated his father as a teenager. That is the insanity into which the Great Sadness throws us.

Self-forgiveness is a controversial topic. Many believe it is too tied to self-help and self-esteem pop psychology, and others believe it is a reflection of pride and lack of faith. There is no text in Scripture that explicitly commands self-forgiveness, so it is said, and only God can forgive. Others, however, genuinely punish themselves by denying themselves self-compassion. They feel a need for self-forgiveness, and their lives are stuck in cycles of guilt, depression, and self-hatred. I have been stuck in that cycle myself in the past—and it still raises its ugly head on occasion.

At one level self-forgiveness, in the strictest terms, is not what we need. What we need is divine forgiveness. What some call self-forgiveness is, I believe, actually the process of accepting God's forgiveness and removing the barriers to that acceptance which burden our hearts. In this sense, I think, self-forgiveness is an expression of a biblical notion of self-love grounded in God's gracious forgiveness and unfailing love. But we cannot receive and feel that grace if we erect walls between God and our true selves.

How do people forgive themselves? I wish I knew. Okay, I have some ideas, but I don't know how to let it sink into my soul. I still have days where I want to beat myself up over my divorce. I still feel a deep sense of failure over it, and sometimes I still feel the guilt associated with that failure, even though I know in my head that God has forgiven me.

I do recognize the insanity of my occasional foray into self-affliction. My self-worth is not found in my perfection, or in my ability to keep the law, or even in a perfect marriage. My self-worth is found in the delight God has for me. God welcomes me and loves me deeply.

On one occasion, when I was shaming myself for my sins, a friend asked an empowering question. "Do you believe God has forgiven you?" Yes, of course, I answered. "So, do you know something God doesn't?" I recognized the point immediately, at least intellectually. When I fail to forgive myself, I make myself god. I become the judge. Whereas God has declared me "free," I continue to bind myself to my sins. What I forgive in others and what God forgives in me, I find difficult to forgive in myself. That is nothing but arrogance and ingratitude. But forgiving oneself is easier said than done.

What hinders self-forgiveness? Here is a partial list, and I'm sure others could add more items out of their own experience. These are some reasons we find it difficult to forgive ourselves. They all fall under the broad rubric of *pride.*

- Continuing the sinful behaviors even when we don't want to (which is the nature of addiction)
- Fearing we will do them again and again given our past failures
- Burying our unresolved guilt so that it becomes a festering wound
- "Fixing it" by doing enough good stuff to restore the balance
- Shaming ourselves with our perfectionism—our expectation that we are better than that; we should have known better and done better

- Lacking trust in God's love because we feel unworthy of love
- Judging ourselves harshly because that is how we have judged others, others have judged us, and thus we judge ourselves
- Directing anger toward ourselves over past behaviors, which leads to self-punishment

If self-forgiveness is actually the acceptance of God's gracious forgiveness, then it is about relationship with God, about being with God, and accepting God's love. Here is a partial list of what that might entail as we move from intellectual acceptance of grace to the authentic experience of grace in our hearts. This will yield self-forgiveness through a healthy self-love because of what God has done.

- Confess our sin to God and trust the promise of forgiveness (1 John 1:9)
- Seek transformation through spiritual disciplines that instill a hope for recovery
- Recognize our unrealistic perfectionistic expectations (let go of self-anger)
- Confess sin mutually in a supportive, safe community of believers
- Make amends to those we have hurt
- Accept responsibility for sin and its consequences (let go of "making up" for sin)
- Pray, contemplating the nature of God, who is full of mercy, compassion, and love
- Meditate and visualize God's word to us: "You are beloved"

Should we forgive ourselves? Yes! Not because this arises out of our own self-will, self-esteem, or self-worth. Rather, we forgive ourselves because God has already forgiven us and we have accepted that forgiveness, which gives us worth, joy, and authentic love. We forgive ourselves because God is greater than our hearts, and God has received us as beloved children.

Our need for self-forgiveness is generated by our prideful rejection of God's forgiveness—our pride that somehow we think we know ourselves better than God does! Such pride is expressed in words like these—which I have said to myself: "How can God forgive me for that when I knew better?" After all, my mind thinks, if you really knew me, you would not forgive me either. Consequently, it is difficult for me to believe that God forgives me or that anyone else could forgive me. Yet, God does. And others have as well. This is the wonder of grace, the joy of being loved even when I feel unlovable.

Pride refuses to accept, internalize, and authentically feel that love. Grace—the active, dynamic, experiential love of God—can heal our wounds if we will but open our hearts to it and let go of the pride. The movement from pride to acceptance is a process, a journey of faith, through which God heals us and transforms us into the likeness of Christ, the image of God.

So, strictly, I suppose we do not forgive ourselves, but rather God forgives us. When we accept that forgiveness deep within our gut, then we can let go of the self-punishment, self-hatred, and fear of failure. Then we are equipped, by God's grace, to give to others what God has given to us.

Forgiving God

God has wronged me . . .
though I cry "Violence," I get no response . . .
his anger burns against me;
he counts me among his enemies.

JOB 19:6, 7, 11

To forgive God is, for many, if not most, a necessary
bridge to praising God. But it is a difficult concept. How does
one forgive God? What does that mean? It sounds blasphe-
mous . . . as if God has done something wrong that needs forgiveness. And who are we to forgive God anyway? We are the
creatures, God is the Creator; we are the clay, God is the Potter.

Bear with me for a bit here.

Mack blames God. He becomes the accuser, thereby taking
on the role of the accuser (Satan). He assaults the goodness

and honesty of God. His anger boils against the One who did not protect Missy. Mack, it seems, must learn to "forgive" God. *The Shack* does not use this language, but the idea is present.

Forgiving God is a controversial topic among many believers, especially Christians. Jewish believers—dating back at least into the early medieval period—have a long history of talking about "forgiving God." In the aftermath of the Holocaust it has become one of the most significant questions in Jewish theology. Can believers forgive God for the death of millions and the seeming failure of God's promises?

When Rabbi Kushner adopted J. B.'s position from Archibald MacLeish's modern retelling of the Job drama, he suggested humans need to forgive God in order to move on with their lives. We need to forgive God for not making a more perfect world. After all, in Kushner's understanding, God is limited—God can't do anything about evil in the world or heal diseases. To forgive God, then, is to recognize God's limitations and not expect more than God can deliver.

This is not, however, what I mean by "forgiving God." It is not to forgive God's limitations or unrighteous acts. The transcendent God does not have inherent limitations, and God is holy without any darkness. Forgiveness, in the sense of showing mercy toward an imperfection, is not applicable to God. So, what does it mean to "forgive God"?

Initially, I, too, resisted the language. But it has grown on me through the experience of life, the depth of hurt, the lament tradition in Scripture, and recognizing my own resentment toward God as it ebbed and flowed with the pains of life.

"Forgiving God" means letting go of the need to judge God—it is the issue that faced Mack before Sophia. It means letting go of "getting back" at God, of brooding over the seeming unfairness of it all. That kind of resentment and bitterness not only stalls spiritual growth. It can kill it. Instead of holding a grudge against God, we let it go.

My anger with God has led to self-pity and resentment. I have, at times, felt "picked on" by God. I have railed against God with the angry but despairing cry, "This is just too much." I understand that anger, and I cannot simply pretend like it is not there (though I have tried that, stuffing it down into my soul). But anger is not the problem—anger should be vented, expressed, prayed. Rather, it is the deep mistrust that sometimes accompanies anger, which turns it into resentment.

While some turn to God in praise and thanksgiving in the midst of their hurt, others turn to God in anger and lament. They are disappointed with God. Like Job, they believe (or at least to them it looks like) God has wronged them. They are frustrated with God's hidden purposes; they are irritated by seemingly meaningless pain. It depresses some and creates anxiety in everyone.

There is, of course, nothing wrong with anger and lament. It is modeled in Scripture. The Hebrew book Job is a dramatic lament. Half of the Psalm-worship of Israel was lament, much of it filled with depression, anger, and confusion. Even the martyred saints around the throne of God ask the classic lament question, "How long?" (Rev. 6:10).

Thus, while some respond with praise and others with lament, both are appropriate and understandable. Indeed, most of those, if not all, who respond with praise also learn to lament as a healthy way of grieving. Saints often move from praise to lament and ultimately—we hope—back to praise.

However, the return to praise is not an easy road. It is filled with potholes and stalked by robbers. For seasons of time some, including myself, turn to bitterness rather than back to praise. In this bitterness, we dwell in our resentment. We project onto God all the inner demons of our own souls. We blame God for all the hurt and pain in our lives. We envy those who have it better; we resent the God who would permit our pain. We doubt, question, and wonder why.

Stuck in bitterness, some ultimately reject God. They move from faith to doubt to unbelief. They rebel against and curse the God they once trusted. I believe this move from bitterness to unbelief is ultimately driven by our own inner wounds, perhaps our own unresolved anger and alienation. When we project our "stuff" (parental abandonment or what-ever it might be) onto God, then we make a God in the image of our wounds or even equate God with our wounds. And who wants that kind of God? It is better to live without a God than to live with that one.

Forgiving God is my language for the process that moves us from bitterness back to praise. Perhaps "forgiving God" is not the best language to use—it is subject to misunderstanding. But "forgiveness," at its heart, is release. To forgive God is to let go of the resentment, to let go of God's throat and of our demand that God treat us as we think we deserve (which, by the way, is a dangerous thing to demand of God—do we really want what we deserve?).

Acceptance is the key. To accept our reality—that is, to live life on its own terms, to take life as it comes—is necessary for comfort and peace in the midst of tragic circumstances. Trusting God generates this acceptance.

Trusting God arises out of contemplating divine greatness—God is God, not me. It arises out of contemplating divine sovereignty—God is in control, not me. It arises out of contemplating divine wisdom—God knows better than I. But, most importantly, this trust arises out of contemplating God's faithful love—I am beloved by God. I will not trust a God who does not love me, but once I am convinced that God loves me more than I love myself, I will trust that God. And this is the God of Jesus—the God of the Cross.

When I trust God, I can forgive God. When I trust God, I can accept my reality. I can let go of control and power. I can let go of my pride that believes I could run the world much better than God does. I can let go of judgment and accept the truth of my circumstances. But my acceptance is contingent upon trusting God's love for me and God's sovereign purposes. And trust is learned—through knowing the Story, living the Story, and experiencing the Story through God's people.

This trusting acceptance is forgiveness—it releases us from our own resentments, bitterness, and self-inflicted wounds. Forgiveness then empowers us to praise God once again, and through praise we experience transformation.

This has been my experience. When hurt and pained, I lament (sometimes with anger). My lament can easily turn to bitterness and resentment. But recalling the Story of God in Jesus, seeking the face of God, and trusting God's love for me, I accept (to one degree or another) my lot and release the resentment. Forgiving God, I learn again to praise God.

Only recently have I realized that this is a constant cycle in my life. Something triggers me, and the cycle begins again.

But, I trust and hope, it is a spiral toward transformation rather than a degenerative plunge into unbelief.

When Mack blamed and resented God and was willing to simply give up on God (Mack: "I'm done, God"), it was because he distrusted God's goodness and purposes. When trust re-enters his soul, he lets go of the blame-game; he lets go of the resentment. This is "forgiving" God.

Trust conquers fear, faith triumphs over resentment, and love does not blame.

CHAPTER 13

Forgiving God: A Testimony

A heart of peace gives life to the body,
but envy rots the bones.

PROVERBS 14:30

One Saturday evening in late 2008, my wife and I attended a fifth-to-eighth-grade talent show at the Lipscomb Campus School—now Lipscomb Academy—in Nashville, Tennessee. It was almost three hours long; yes, that long.

About thirty minutes into the program, I began to feel uncomfortable.

Something was gnawing at me. My insides were pushing me to run, to get out of the building, to find a way to excuse myself. Something was telling me that if I could just go home, I could regain my serenity. A year previous, that is probably what I would have done, but that serenity would have been an illusion, an escape.

This night, however, I turned inward. The problem was not the program but something going on inside of me. As the program proceeded, I began to meditate, calm myself, and pray. I wanted to know what was really festering in me. The kids were doing their best, and they weren't so bad that I needed to escape—some of them were actually very good. There was something else I wanted to escape. I needed to sit in my feelings, discern what was happening, and feel my way through the mess that was my soul.

As I meditated, I became aware of my envy. I did not envy the children. I envied the parents. I noticed that I was agitated by their joy and the wonder of their eyes. I was particularly annoyed by how much the family behind me was enjoying their star's performance. They, of course, did not cause my anxiety. Rather, my own wounds generated it. This was not about them; it was about me.

Envy. Not envious of talent, money, power, or job, but envious that these parents were blessed by God to watch their children perform. I was never able to do that with Joshua. When he was the age of these children, he was in a wheelchair, could barely walk, and spent most of his time unaware of his surroundings.

Judgment too! Did these parents really fully enjoy what their kids were doing? Did they understand how blessed they were?

From six to sixteen my family watched Joshua slowly die. I never saw Joshua play a team sport, never saw him perform on a stage, never saw him read a poem, or read at all! I never even saw him color between the lines. I envied the parents and begrudged their joy, and—in my harsh and unkind judgment—wondered whether they truly appreciated their blessing.

But that was not the root. Resentment was the root of my feeling that night; that was my discomfort—my need for escape. I wanted to run away so I would not have to think about my pain, about Joshua's illness and death. I did not want to acknowledge my resentment. I would rather not think about it or feel it. It was easier to simply escape, to flee.

I did not resent the parents. I resented the God who blessed these children but not Joshua. God gave these gifts to these parents, but I was never able to enjoy those gifts with Joshua. Presumably, they had prayed for healthy children, and so had I!

I had missed out, and there was no one to blame except God. Is God not responsible for this world? Did we not pray that we would have a healthy son? Why did God say, "No, he won't be healthy"? I resent that answer, I protest it, and sometimes I'm not sure I can put up with a God like that.

Even as I write these words, I know I received many gifts from Joshua, and they were divine blessings. Even as I think again about his broken body, I still remember his smile, his laugh, and the joy of sitting him on my lap in my big chair, watching one of his favorite movies (*The Wizard of Oz*). I realize I was blessed, but that Saturday evening, I resented that God had not blessed me more richly—that he had not blessed me like those parents in that auditorium that night.

As I meditated on that resentment, I noted my feelings.

Irritation.

Frustration.

Anger.

Envy.

Jealousy.

Resentment.

And I took them to God. I told God how I felt. I let it out so I could let it go, so I could release it into God's hands. I needed to be heard . . . by God! And, in being heard, I could let go . . . at least for that night. In that moment, I could "forgive" God.

In letting go, I could remember the blessings I did receive through Joshua. I could treasure those and hold them in my heart. And I could thank God for them. I could value the experiences—the learning and growth experienced in the process. I could even see God in many of those painful moments—God present to comfort in my laments, God present through people who served my family, God present in laughter as well as tears.

That night—at least for that night—I forgave God. In releasing my resentment, I was given some peace and joy. Bit by bit, day by day, little by little, the comfort is renewed and joy returns.

I am grateful for God's patience with me. Even when I am filled with bitter resentment, God loves me, graciously receives my forgiveness (which, of course, he does not need it!), and is not frustrated with me when the resentment returns on a cold Saturday night in December seven-and-a-half years after Joshua's death.

Thank you, Yahweh. Truly, your loving kindness endures forever.

CHAPTER 14

Designed for Intimacy

He took Peter, James and John along with him,
and he began to be deeply distressed and troubled.
"My soul is crushed with sorrow to the point of death,"
he said to them. "Stay here and keep watch."

MARK 14:33–34

The Great Sadness changed Mack. Previous to it, he was friendly, and though he was mostly superficial in his conversations, he was nevertheless engaged with the world around him. But the Great Sadness changed that.

Mack became more and more isolated. He stopped "going to church" (for the most part) and no longer hung out with his longtime friend Willie. He no longer looked anyone in the eye. The hurt, shame, and darkness of the Great Sadness burdened him. He was emotionally shut down and shut off from everyone else.

Great Sadness has the tendency to isolate people, and those burdened with it have a tendency to withdraw—physically, emotionally, and spiritually. They become loners in their inner souls, as no one is permitted to enter, see, or know their shacks.

But Mack's experience with Papa, Jesus, and Sarayu changed that. We see it in the way he talks with Jesus. As he walks with Jesus, Mack talks about his fears, tears, and cheers. They walk together as if they are in a relationship, an intimate one where they share experiences and feelings. Mack was learning to be intimate as Jesus led him into those uncertain waters.

We might say that Jesus has had lots of practice. Jesus lived with twelve disciples whom he called friends. He traveled with the twelve, ate with the twelve, taught the twelve, sent the twelve out to herald the good news and heal the sick, and prayed with the twelve. There were times when he prayed with them (Luke 9:18) and times when he prayed alone (Luke 6:12–13). But there were other times when Jesus prayed with only three.

We might compare the twelve to a kind of task-oriented small group. It was training ground for the twelve, and Jesus was their discipler and teacher, but the three were something different. In a group of three or four, intimacy can happen in ways that do not usually happen in a group of twelve or more.

Intimacy defies definition. It is a subjective, personal experience of being in relation with another. It enables one to actually see into the other: "into-me-see" or intimacy. It is sharing ourselves, our experiences, our feelings, our secrets, our lives. It is letting another person into our real selves—letting them see how we truly see ourselves. We let them come into our shacks.

Obviously, intimacy needs safety; intimacy only happens in safe places with safe people. It only happens when there is trust. And it usually only happens within a small group (three to eight people) or with a few individuals.

Jesus built this kind of intimacy with Peter, James, and John. He shared life with them in more intimate ways than he did with the twelve. He took them places and did things with them that he did not do with all twelve. Jesus built an intimate trust with these three. In fact, this relationship models how we ourselves might develop intimates.

We build intimacy with others through shared experiences (Luke 8:51). He shared something with them that deepened their friendship and developed intimacy. We partner with each other in a task or spend time with each other in personal, tragic, or thrilling moments. Through shared experiences, we learn to trust each other as we see each other coping with reality. Shared experiences develop trust.

We build intimacy with others through shared strength (Luke 9:28–29). As Jesus faced his final journey to Jerusalem, he needed affirmation and blessing, and God provided it: "This is my Son whom I love." Jesus brought the three with him as a small prayer group, and God showed up. Together, as an intimate group, the four are strengthened, renewed, and affirmed by the divine Presence. Jesus finds strength in a divine Presence experienced in community with his intimate friends.

We build intimacy with others through shared feelings (Mark 14:33–34). Jesus had just come from an emotional last supper with the twelve and had come to the Garden of Gethsemane with the eleven. Walking with the three deeper into the garden, Jesus begins to feel the enormity of what is about to happen.

His spirit is troubled—even frightened—and overwhelmed. Grief and sorrow flood his heart; it crushes him to the point of death. He agonizes over his decision to submit to the will of the Father. Astoundingly, he confesses the depth of his feeling to his intimate friends; he reveals his true self. He shares his feelings with them. He wants his friends to "watch with him"— to share his feelings, to pray with him, to be there for him. He needs a listening ear; he needs the support of his intimates.

Jesus himself needed the intimacy of human companionship, just as he needed to eat, sleep, and rest. He would not be authentically human otherwise. God did not create us to live in isolation from others. Rather, he built into us a bonding mechanism that connects with other people. This can become unhealthy (as in codependency), but connection with other people is necessary for personal, mental, and spiritual health. Humans are meant to live in relation with others just as the Triune God is community-in-relation. When these relationships remain superficial, we lose what God intended intimacy to provide. Without intimacy, we become sick and ultimately die inside.

Human intimacy provides authentic relationship, accountability in living, support in times of need, companions to share joy with, and the ability to live without secrets. Jesus nurtured this kind of intimacy with Peter, James, and John.

The journey into intimacy is difficult and risky. It is sometimes painful—even as it was for Jesus himself when the three disciples could not stay awake to pray with him and then would later deny him. Yet Jesus risked intimacy and shared himself, because any other journey is lonely, fearful, and isolating. We cannot become what God intends without intimacy with others. Without intimacy—at some level—we erect a façade, a Hollywood front, and we live with a divided self. We retreat into our shacks. We let others see one person (a mask), but the real self we keep hidden in the shack.

We really don't want anyone to see us as we really are—we really don't want intimacy with others—because we fear their rejection, disappointment, or betrayal. But we cannot truly be ourselves without others—at least someone—knowing us.

Do we have people with whom we can

- express our deepest and most authentic feelings?
- tell our darkest secrets?
- safely talk about our relationships?
- confess sin?
- let our guard down and be fully real?

Mack learned intimacy by being with the Triune God that weekend. We learn intimacy by being with others. I spend time every week with three different small groups (one with couples and two with just men). I call them my "intimacy groups," and everyone in those groups knows my secrets. They know me. They know my shack.

As long as our shacks remain hidden, we cannot enjoy what God has designed us to become. As long as our shacks remain hidden, we will live in loneliness, isolation, and darkness. God did not design us for that. God invites us to our shacks to share ourselves, to experience divine love, and to become all we were intended to be.

Who knows your shack? All of your shack?

PART II

Encountering GOD in a Fresh Way

What's All the Fuss About?

CHAPTER 15

An African American Female Papa

*There the angel of the LORD appeared to him
in flames of fire from within a bush.*

EXODUS 3:2

One of the most striking features of Young's parable is his depiction of the Father. This has occasioned criticism at several levels.

Is it idolatry to portray the Father in such a manner? Does the female metaphor undermine the biblical image of the Father?

Admittedly, the imagery is startling. To picture the Father as a gregarious African American woman is counterintuitive to most Western Christian sensibilities. Is the Father really so gregarious? Is the Father female? Is the Father African American?

Is the intimacy too chummy, too familiar? Is the holiness—the transcendent distinction of the divine—trumped here?

My take on this literary move by Young is shaped by my understanding of what he is doing in *The Shack*. Young is weaving a story that will help wounded people come to believe God really loves them. Many, like Young himself, were wounded by their fathers. Mack was physically abused by his father and wants nothing to do with him.

A critical moment in the parable is when the door of the shack swings open and Mack meets God. Whose face will he see? What kind of face will he see? How will God greet Mack? If Mack sees his father, then shame, hurt, anger, and pain would fill his heart. Instead, Mack sees a woman of color.

This arises out of Young's own experience, when his earliest memories of love and acceptance were shaped by the dark-skinned women of New Guinea. Those memories and some subsequent relationships with African American women explain why Young portrays Papa as an African American woman. Young is not trying to be politically correct or promoting some kind of "goddess" motif. Rather, he writes out of his own experience of love—where he himself felt loved.

The African American form of the Father in the parable is a metaphor; it is not a one-to-one image of the Father, as if it were an idolatrous substitute for God. It functions as a theophany, not a digital photo. It comes in a vision (a dream; Mack had cried himself to sleep on the floor of the shack).

God appears to Mack as an African American woman because this metaphor or form communicates to Mack how delighted God is to spend time with him. The metaphor overturns some mistaken conceptions of God in Mack's mind—conceptions more rooted in his abusive earthly father than in the God of Scripture. It is a theophany—the appearance of God in a particular form—for the sake of encounter, communication, and connection.

Theophanies are common in Scripture. God comes as three visitors to Abraham's tent. God, in human form, wrestles with Jacob. God comes as a dove descending out of the heavens at the baptism of Jesus. God appears as a burning bush. God is even pictured with hands and feet, sitting on a throne in the Temple's Holy of Holies.

I don't find a theophanic depiction of the Father disturbing. It would be more disturbing (and indebted to Greek philosophy) to ascribe to the Father a kind of transcendence that cannot appear to human beings in a theophany, vision, or dream. This does not detract from the revelation of God in Jesus. In fact, it is consistent with that revelation, as incarnation (God coming in the flesh) moves beyond theophanies.

God comes to people in a way that communicates something about the divine identity. This does not mean the form in which God comes is actually who God is. To identify the form with God is idolatry and fails to recognize how God transcends any form in which God appears. A theophany reveals the divine nature through a particular medium, but the divine nature is not limited to that medium.

This is a brilliant move. I know people who cannot connect with the Father's love because their own fathers were so abusive. If they opened their shacks and saw their fathers, they would hesitate, doubt, and reject the love offered. Their hearts would leap with fear rather than delight. But if they opened their shacks and saw how God had come to them in a form (theophany, metaphor) which connects with loving experiences in their own life, then they would more readily embrace the love offered. God meets us in our personal experiences in ways that best communicate divine love and in ways that we might best experience that love.

That God appears as a woman is not a huge stretch. Jesus himself told a parable that pictured the Father as a woman searching for a lost coin (Luke 15:8–10), analogous to the father who waited for his lost son to appear in the parable of the Prodigal Son. Scripture often uses feminine metaphors to describe God's love for Israel (cf. Isa. 49:15; 66:13) and even describes God as both the One who fathers us and the One who gives us birth (Deut. 32:18). Young simply uses the metaphor in an extended way to make the same point biblical authors make. It is a theophany of divine love.

God, of course, is neither African American nor Asian nor Western. God, of course, is neither male nor female, neither black nor white. God transcends and at the same time encompasses such categories. Masculinity and femininity are both aspects of the divine nature since we—both male and female—were created in the image of God. Whether black or white or red or yellow—as we sing in the children's song, the diverse ethnicity and colors are also aspects of God's own diversity (the Trinity) and divine love for the diverse character of the creation. God created diversity! It is part of God's original intent for the world.

Young recognizes the relative way in which God appears as an African American woman by changing the form when Papa leads Mack to Missy's body. On that day, Mack needed a father; that is, he needed the human—even male—qualities fathers represent, and Papa comes to him as male. The form in which God appears to Mack is relative to Mack's needs, as God seeks to commune and communicate with him.

The truth is this: God is delighted to meet us at our shacks. Young communicates this through a feminine African American metaphor for the Father, because it is what Mack needs (and how Young experienced recovery as he connected with those early experiences of love from the indigenous women of New Guinea).

I find it helpful to use different metaphors for God as I envision God's delight for me and experience the comfort of God's enveloping love—something I am still learning to do. Whether it is crawling into my mother's lap or a bear-hug from my brother, it communicates something true about the Father where an image of a male parent might not always do the same thing emotionally and spiritually. My favorite metaphor for the God who greets me at my shack is the image of Joshua sleeping in my arms as he rests on my lap in my big chair.

The Shack's metaphor is bold and daring but enriching and redemptive for those who connect with it, given their own particular experiences.

Our imagination, guided by Scripture and sanctified by the Spirit, is an important tool for letting the truth that God loves us sink into our hearts, into our gut. During my devotional time, I envision the Father, Son, and Spirit meeting with me. They are delighted that I have come to listen to them and talk with them. They welcome me. My imagination becomes a means by which I experience, by the power of the Spirit, the love of the Triune God.

The Shack has given many believers the resources to imagine—to visualize in their minds—their own encounter with God for the sake of imbibing God's love and letting it settle into their hearts. The Spirit uses our imagination—our dreams, art, and poetry—for that purpose, just as the Spirit uses preaching, assembled praise, and the sacraments (baptism and the Lord's Supper) as well. The Spirit, through metaphors, images, other people, and the sacraments, impresses our hearts with the truth that the Father loves us and that we are God's beloved in whom God delights.

CHAPTER 16

Intimacy with Papa: Renaming God?

*The Spirit you received does not make you slaves,
so that you live in fear again; rather the Spirit you
received brought about your adoption to sonship. And
by him we cry, "Abba, Father." The Spirit himself
testifies with our spirit that we are God's children.*

ROMANS 8:15–16

One of the more striking dimensions of *The Shack* is the intimate picture Young paints of Mack's relationship with the Triune God. This intimacy is portrayed through actions (eating, gardening, and cooking with God), language (Papa), and settings (lake, log cabin, garden). Relationality is at the heart of this picture as God lives in relationship with Mack, the kind of relationship that is fully and personally engaged in every aspect of Mack's being.

It seems obvious to me that "Papa" is a modernized English version of "Abba," an Aramaic term for "my father." But "Papa" may communicate something not in the Aramaic term "Abba." A common misunderstanding is that "Abba" is a diminutive form of "Father" such as "Daddy" or "Papa." "Abba," however, actually is a respectful direct address that also expresses intimacy—perhaps something like "my dear father." It expresses intimacy with respect and honor.

As a consequence, I'm not too enthused about "Papa" as a form of address to God in my own prayer life or when I'm talking about God, since it can lack a sense of honor or reverence (depending on how it is heard or used). But I understand the point Young wants to make. He wants to lead us into a kind of familial kinship with God. And, indeed, we should embrace that kind of relationship with the Triune God. "Papa" works as a metaphor for intimacy, but unintended consequences or implications may render its usefulness in liturgy or theology suspect. It can reduce God to a "papa" (a human conceptualization)—but so can any human word if we remove it from the context of the novel itself or the context of a broader theology (who God is).

Context is important here. Young seeks to reconnect wounded people with the God who they believe, in some sense, wounded them. Consequently, an emphasis on intimacy, relationality, and familiarity is important for healing. Wounded people need to experience the delight God has for them, the ease with which God converses with them, and the friendliness of God. Within this context and purpose, "Papa" works as a metaphor.

At this point, it would be easy to critique the way Young portrays how chummy God is with Mack. While watching Papa, Jesus, and Sarayu converse with Mack, one could easily forget about God's transcendent otherness, God's holy distinctiveness. But this would be unfair to Young's purpose.

There are moments when Papa reminds Mack that this appearance does not mean that now Mack can fully grasp God's identity. For example, Papa tells Mack, "I am far more than that, above and beyond all that you can ask or think" (100), and it is a "good thing" that Mack cannot "grasp the wonder" of God's nature (103). This is a healthy emphasis on divine transcendence.

But despite such caveats and the parabolic context, nagging discomfort remains for some. I understand that discomfort. I feel it a bit myself. I feel it because I sense that sufficient acknowledgement of the holiness of God may be missing in the book. What I mean by holiness is not God's ethical perfection, but God's otherness and distinctiveness (cf. Psalm 99:1–3). It is the kind of holiness that demands Moses to take off his shoes before the theophany of the burning bush (Ex. 3). It is the kind of holiness that evokes a confession of sin from Isaiah before the throne of God (Isa. 6). This is generally missing in the novel. And yet, at the same time, I understand why it is missing: wounded people initially need divine intimacy rather than divine transcendence for their healing.

A corollary of this missing sense of divine holiness is the absence of the wrath of God in the work. But is it totally absent? It is absent in that the fire of God does not consume sinful people in the book (and that is not an image wounded people need to hear initially), but it is not absent in the sense that God holds Mack accountable at every point. Mack is not let off the hook. He is confronted, particularly in the chapter where Sophia questions him. Mack is forced to face judgment in the sense that he has to face himself and acknowledge the truth about himself.

At the same time, we should remember the language of divine friendship is present in Scripture. Job, for example, spoke of "God's intimate friendship" in the days prior to his suffering (Job 29:4). Abraham is described as God's "friend" in several places (2 Chron. 20:7; Isa. 41:8; Jas. 2:23). Jesus calls his disciples "friends" (John 15:14). Moreover, since the marriage metaphor is so often used to describe God's relationship with Israel, "intimates" as well as "friends" is an appropriate description of how God enjoys relationship with others.

Young's focus on intimacy and relationship is healthy for wounded people. It is not the whole story, and there is no claim that the parable tells the whole story. This parable is no more the whole story than the Prodigal Son is the whole story. But it has a significant and important point to make about intimacy.

Intimacy is what religion addicts and performance-oriented believers lack. We do the rituals, follow the rules, and pursue good works for approval or out of duty. This ultimately wounds us by shaping us into people who emphasize rules rather than relationships. And when the other wounds of life come, it provides little comfort. Rather, we take our licks, continue our performance, and hide a nagging sense of God's unfairness in our hearts. Since we have little or no relationship or intimacy with God—even though we think we do!—we pull ourselves up by our bootstraps and keep on keeping on. We persevere in our duty.

That kind of perseverance, however, turns into bitterness and meanness. We are upset that others are not performing like we perform. We are bitter that we are wounded despite our good performances. We become unforgiving, unmerciful, and unhappy—we will treat others the way we think God has treated us, or at least as other religion addicts have treated us. Nevertheless, we keep doing our duty because we are religion addicts.

Intimacy is the path of healing for addicts. Intimacy with God—eating with God at the table—heals wounds. It is not the only aspect of God, nor should we reduce God to some human conception of intimacy, but it is a necessary part of healing from our wounds. Intimacy brings joy in the midst of hurt. Intimacy displays God's delight in us. Intimacy brings forgiveness, mercy, and joy.

In that context, the metaphor Papa works for me. God has invited me into the circle of Triune love to enjoy the familial reality that is the communion of the Triune God. God rejoices and sings over me, *even in my shack*! Wow!

Thanks, Papa.

CHAPTER 17

Three and One: Trinitarian Heresy?

May the grace of the Lord Jesus Christ,
and the love of God, and the fellowship
of the Holy Spirit be with you all.

2 CORINTHIANS 13:14

The portrayal of the Trinity in *The Shack* has come under two assaults from critics. Some suggest that *The Shack* teaches modalism, while others believe it teaches tritheism (both of these ideas are defined below). The fact that such polar opposite accusations are present in the blogosphere indicates . . . well, it is interesting, to say the least. Perhaps it is more in the eye (or agenda) of the critic than in the text of the novel.

Modalism is an ancient heresy which affirms that the one God comes to us as Father, Son, and Spirit, as three functions

119

rather than three persons. Father, Son, and Spirit are merely different modes of revelation or different hats the one God wears. There are no personal distinctions between the Father, Son, and Spirit. Rather, God is one person who appears in different ways at different times. Ultimately, the Father is the same person as the Son, and the Spirit is the same person as the Father, and the Son is the same person as the Spirit. There are no real, personal distinctions or individuations of any kind within the one God. There is no real threeness—"three" is only an appearance, a mask God wears at different times.

Tritheism is another ancient heresy which few, if any, ever affirmed, but the early church wanted to avoid it. It affirms that God is a triad of three independent beings, as if three gods came together to work on an agreed plan of action. They formed a kind of corporation to accomplish a task together. There is no union in substance or essence but only in purpose and goal. They are three autonomous gods who decided to work together.

Trinitarianism (Christian Orthodoxy epitomized in the Nicean Creed) has always sought to avoid both extremes, though not always successfully. I think *The Shack* wants to avoid those extremes as well. It is hard to see modalism when all three sit at the table eating with Mack, and he has distinct personal conversations with each. Tritheism seems more likely, because threeness is emphasized in *The Shack*. But Young is also careful to stress the unity, mutual interdependence, and shared consciousness of Papa, Jesus, and Sarayu—their total transparency, deference, and shared life are intended to communicate oneness.

Young is neither a modalist nor a tritheist in intent. Papa's statement to Mack clearly rejects both:

We are not three gods [tritheism], and we are not talking about one god with three attitudes [modalism], like a man who is a husband, father, and worker [wearing different hats]. I am one God and I am three persons, and each of the three is fully and entirely the one (103).

Young's formulation is a classic statement of Trinitarianism: one God in three persons.

What are we to make of this? What is important here theologically? What generates confusion? Why is this important for the message of *The Shack*?

The accusation of modalism is often rooted in Papa's wounds. In Young's parable, the Father has stigmata, the wounds of the cross, on her body. This is, supposedly, evidence of Patripassianism (a form of modalism), which claims the Father suffered on the cross, as if the Father and Son were the same person rather than distinct persons.

I think this accusation misses the point, and thus it misses one of the key healing motifs the parable embraces. The scars are not about modalism, but about the experience of the Father through the incarnation of the Son. The Father suffers through the Son rather than suffering as the Son (which would be modalistic Patripassianism—that is, the suffering of the Father on the cross). The Father dwells in the Son as the Son suffers, and thus the Father suffers as well. In that sense, as Papa says, "we were there *together*" (98). The Father was in Christ reconciling the world to himself (2 Cor. 5:19).

This is an important point. The Father empathizes with humanity through the Son. Mack wonders how Papa could ever understand how he feels, and then he sees the wounds on Papa as tears trickled down her face. When Jesus suffered, the Triune God—including the Father—suffered through him, because the Son participates in the divine community and the divine community is transparent with each other. Jesus's human experience becomes the experience of the Father through the shared consciousness of the Triune God. This does not mean that the Father became flesh or experienced flesh independently of the Son, nor does it mean that the Father died on the cross, but the Father did enter into human experience *through* the suffering of the Son by means of the shared consciousness (the oneness) of the Father, Son, and Spirit.

A populist understanding of atonement tends to distance the Father from the suffering of the Son. The Father is the punisher, and the Son persuades the Father to accept sinners. The wounds on Papa are a corrective to this populist misunderstanding. When Mack was angry about how broken the world is, he asked, "Why doesn't he do something about it?" "He already has," Sophia answered. "Haven't you seen the wounds on Papa, too?" (166). The Father suffered—the whole Trinity suffered—through the death of Jesus, and they suffered for the sake of mercy and out of their love. This is not modalism; this is good pastoral theology.

Tritheism, it seems to me, is the more problematic accusation. The problem in describing a theophanic encounter with the Father, Son, and Spirit is the seeming individualization of the Father, Son, and Spirit. Human language is limited in its attempt to approximate the transcendent reality of the Triune relationship and its oneness. Anytime we describe this relationship with human metaphors (e.g., African American Papa, Asian Sarayu, dove?, etc.) we risk reducing the Trinity to those metaphors. Anytime we talk about the Father, Son, and Spirit as distinct individuations or persons, we risk tritheism.

But Scripture itself does this. Threeness can certainly appear tritheistic at the baptism of Jesus—the Father's voice, Jesus in the water, and the dove (Holy Spirit) descending. John 14–17 can be read in a tritheistic way—there are clearly three identities with their own personal pronouns, distinct from the others, as Father, Son, and Spirit. At the same time, in John 14–17, there is unity of nature, purpose, and communion through mutual indwelling.

The fundamental problem, I think, is that the unity of the three persons of the Trinity far transcends any human ability to imagine. Modern Westerners live so individualistically and look at the world with such compartmentalization that the substantial and communal unity of three persons is inconceivable. In reality, it is indescribable, as the finite human mind cannot grasp the transcendent unity of God in three persons.

Theophanies will naturally tend toward individuation, but they are theophanies, not the reality of God within God's own life. So, we should give Young a break here, just as we see Scripture doing something similar in the three friends who visit Abraham. Human language cannot fully describe or portray the one God in three persons. Theophanies are impressionistic paintings—meant to make an impression on us; they are not digital photographs.

The Shack seeks to maintain the Trinitarian balance of "oneness" and "threeness." Whether it does or not is subject

Trinity: A Circle of Love

I have given them the glory that you gave me, that
they may be one as we are one—I in them and you in
me—so they may be brought to complete unity. Then
the world will know that you sent me and have loved
them even as you have loved me. . . . I have made you
known to them, and will continue to make you known
in order that the love you have for me may be in them
and that I myself may be in them.

JOHN 17:22–23, 26

Mack, to say the least, is startled by the way God appeared to him in the shack—an African American woman, an Asian personality, and a Jewish man (no European among them). Confused, Mack asked, "Which one of you is God?" "I am," they all answered (89). All three are "I AM"—they are all God.

It is a striking picture. If we focus entirely on the gender and ethnicity of the theophanic representations (though they have a point), we will miss what is at the real heart of Young's parable.

The Triune God is a "*circle* of relationship" (124). The content or experience of this relationship is itself love. God is love—it is the experience of the Father, Son, and Spirit in relationship. They—their relationship, their being-in-relation—is love. The Trinity is a community; God is a community. And God is love.

Perhaps if we want to identify the kind of Trinitarianism present in *The Shack*, it comes closest to the Social Trinitarianism of the Eastern church, particularly the Cappadocians, and it is embraced by many prominent modern theologians. One important aspect of this conception of the Trinity is the social relation between the persons of the Trinity. They exist in a communion of relationship in which they experience what the Greek church has called *perichoresis*.

Don't be frightened by this Greek word, but embrace it. It offers a powerful picture of God. You might recognize *peri* as part of many English terms like *perimeter* or *periscope*. It means "around" or in the round, a circle. *Choresis* is present in English words like *choreography* and means "dance." Imagine a Greek wedding (like in *My Big Fat Greek Wedding*) where the guests dance in a circle holding hands. This is the Trinitarian dance—a circle of love which is filled with joy, transparency, and intimacy.

The perichoretic Trinity lives in a harmonious community as being-in-relation; they live in transparency and in sync with each other as one. They interpenetrate each other—they mutually indwell and coinhere each other. The one God lives in a relational community, in a circle of love, in a beautiful and wondrous dance of love. Their oneness far exceeds any vision of oneness humans can muster, but their relationship is exactly what we were created to embody in our communal life. We are to become one just as they are one.

This is what, I think, Young pictures in *The Shack*. Clearly, it is an accommodative, metaphorical picture. It is art, not science.

This kind of Trinitarian picture is part of historic Eastern Orthodox iconography. One of the most famous is Rublev's "Holy Trinity" (1410). The icon portrays Abraham's three visitors as the Trinity (Genesis 18:1 says that "the Lord appeared to Abraham"). The icon paints this theophany. Here, as in Young's story, we have three sitting at a table communing with each other but also inviting us to commune with them. Notice how the bowl on the table invites viewers to sit at the table with the three and commune with them. We are invited to participate in the divine communion—to join the circle of love, to join the dance.

Young's parable is a literary form of what that icon pictures. It is far from heretical. Rather, it is a parabolic portrayal of Social Trinitarianism, which the Eastern church has affirmed for centuries.

But why is this important to Young? What does this have to do with our shacks?

Wounded people tend to isolate. Addicts immerse themselves in their own shame and feel unloved. Trinitarian theology is extremely important for the wounded and the addict, because Social Trinitarianism emphasizes the relationality and communion of love between the three persons. What *The Shack* offers wounded people is a vision of the loving relationship into which they are invited. This is who God is—the lover who yearns to bear-hug us and wants us to experience loving communion. Wounded people want to be loved. They need to be loved. They want to feel loved. This is not an abstract idea but a dynamic, real communing between the Father, Son, and Spirit.

The Father loved the Son before the foundation of the world, and the Father loves us just as he loves his own Son (John 17:23–24). The mission of God is to include us in the circle of *perichoretic* love. The love the Father, Son, and Spirit have for each other is exactly the love God wants us to experience in our relationship with the divine community. The mission of God is that "the love with which" the Father "loved" the Son "may be in" us and they in us (John 17:26). As Jesus tells Mack, humans were "always intended to be [in] the very center of our love and our purpose." God's goal is to dwell in and with humanity, and for humanity to dwell in God.

That is truly amazing! It is the good news of the gospel. Though the world is broken and filled with pain, though I am wounded and sinful, the good news is that God places me at the center of his love and purpose. The good news is that, no matter what my shack may look like, I am loved!

I see myself at the center of God's love. The Father, Son, and Spirit, joined hand-in-hand, form a circle of love, and they dance around me. I stand in the middle of their circle as the Triune God dances around me, rejoices over me, and pours their love into my heart. The Father, Son, and Spirit sing over me as I bask in the sunlight of their love.

CHAPTER 19

An Asian Holy Spirit?

*May the God of hope fill you with all joy and peace
as you trust in him, so that you may overflow
with hope by the power of the Holy Spirit.*

ROMANS 15:13

Sarayu is a Hindi word, a language spoken in India. Some have thought that Young is subtly introducing Hinduism into Christianity or introducing some kind of religious pluralism. But the truth is much more innocuous.

As Young has told the story on many occasions (check his talks on the Internet), he was baffled by what name to give the Holy Spirit in his parable. He knew he wanted a name that meant "wind," which is exactly what both the Hebrew (*ruach*) and Greek (*pneuma*) words translated "Spirit" mean. While engaged in a job-related conversation with a tech in India, he asked her what they called "wind" in India. She gave him several different names, but when she used the term *sarayu*, his ears perked up. It sounded good, but to what kind of wind did it refer? The tech described it as a wind that was unexpected but refreshing, the kind of wind that catches you by surprise—a fresh breeze everyone loves and that makes a hot day bearable. In addition, the word also names a river in India.

Young uses this name because this is exactly what the Spirit is in the life of the believer—a surprising, unpredictable, refreshing breath of God, which forms a river of living water within us. These are the metaphors John uses in his Gospel (John 3:6–8; 7:37–39). Sarayu, the "playful eddying wind," is Young's attempt to visualize the Holy Spirit in the light of the Gospel of John's own metaphors (132).

Since Sarayu is a Hindi name for wind, Young describes him/her—the theophany does not clearly identify the gender of Sarayu, sometimes female, sometimes male—as an Asian breath, an almost ethereal figure that moves gently across a room with blowing hair and shimmering light. Light radiates through her, which gives her the appearance of being in several places at once as she floats from place to place. Sarayu is a sunbeam of love.

How does one describe the Spirit of God, the Holy Spirit? If the Father seems sometimes the most distant (transcendent) of the Triune fellowship, the Spirit seems the most mysterious. Jesus has a face; he is a human being with whom we can identify. The Spirit does not have a face. Fatherhood is a metaphor with which we can connect in terms of our earthly experience. But "Spirit" seems indefinable, indescribable, and imperceptible. Attempting to depict the Spirit in pictorial forms (as the Gospels do with the "dove" at the baptism of Jesus) is a difficult task. Any choice would be subject to criticism, but we also need to listen to what the author is attempting to communicate. If a descending dove was a symbol of the glory of God descending on the obedient Son, what is the symbolism of Sarayu in Young's parable?

Young introduces Sarayu as the collector of tears. "We all have things we value enough to collect, don't we?" she asks (86). Mack collected his valuables in a tin box, which contained, among other things, Missy's picture. Sarayu removes tears from our faces and collects them in her "crystal bottle." She is the Presence of God who wipes our tears, holds them in her heart, and comforts us. The Holy Spirit is the great Comforter who lives within us; the One who groans with us, groans for us, and soothes us with the calm of a mother's touch.

The primary work of the Spirit in *The Shack*, however, is the garden—not just Mack's garden, but all of our gardens. We each have a garden; it is our soul. The garden is a rich metaphor for the Spirit's presence in our lives. The Spirit tends our gardens—weeding, pruning, watering, burning, and creating. Sarayu loves her gardens, takes joy in the work she does, and anticipates (yearns for) the finished product that is never quite complete in the present.

The Spirit, who is the love of God poured into our hearts (Rom. 5:5), is the active gardener producing the fruit of peace, joy, and love in our lives. The Spirit of patience produces patience in our hearts so that we learn to live through (endure) the Great Sadness in our lives. The Spirit of gentleness produces gentleness in us so that we treat others with conviction, kindness, and forgiveness. The Spirit of goodness produces the kind of goodness that embodies the life of God in our lives. These are the "fruits of the Spirit" (Gal. 5:22).

The Spirit produces them, but we cooperate with the Spirit as we "keep in step with the Spirit" (Gal. 5:25). We tend our own gardens as well. The Spirit invites us to help her—just as in the original garden (Eden), God invited humanity to tend the garden as God's own representative (image). But humanity knows how to mess up a garden much better than it knows how to cooperate with God's Spirit. We create our own messes, and other humans trespass in and destroy our gardens.

But God loves us in our messes and continues to tend our gardens, rooting out our wounds and planting fresh flowers to bloom in our hearts. The Spirit is always doing something new in the garden. Sarayu is not yet finished with us; she is a surprising, fresh wind, cooling our warm days.

The presence of Sarayu in our gardens, our souls, is an expression of the intimacy God shares with us. By the Spirit, we cry, "Abba, Father" (Gal. 4:6). We pray through the "love of the Spirit" (Rom. 15:30), which fills our hearts, and we live in the "fellowship of the Spirit" (2 Cor. 13:14). The Spirit is the Presence of God in our hearts—real, authentic, and experiential. The Spirit is always present—always with us.

The constant presence of God is partly the means by which our relationship with God grows and blooms. As that relationship deepens and the Spirit beautifies (sanctifies) our garden more completely, we become ever deeper intimates with God. We come to know God—not simply in cognitive or propositional ways, but we come to know God's own heart and we experience God's life within us and among us.

This is the intimacy Sarayu illuminates when she explains that she wants Mack "to be aware" of her "in a special way." She wants him to "hear" her. Sarayu describes it as learning to hear the Spirit's thoughts in our own thoughts (197). This does not mean human beings become infallible or no longer mistake their own agendas for God's goals. We have done that way too often. But it does mean that slowly, progressively, and ultimately, God shapes our hearts. When our hearts are God-shaped—as the Spirit writes the life of God upon our hearts—we can hear the Spirit's thoughts in our own thoughts. The Spirit helps us become like God.

Sarayu, this surprising Asian theophany, reminds us that the Spirit of God cannot be captured and controlled any more than the wind can. The Spirit blows where he/she wills and surprises us with peace, comfort, and grace in life's most troubled moments. The Spirit surprises us with holiness, which we once thought impossible in our broken shacks.

The God of hope brings hope, renewal, and peace into our hearts by the power of the Holy Spirit.

CHAPTER 20

What If God Were One of Us: Jesus, a Dependent Human?

Who, being in very nature God,
did not consider equality with God
something to be used to his own advantage;
rather, he made himself nothing
by taking the very nature of a servant,
being made in human likeness.
And being found in appearance as a man,
he humbled himself
by becoming obedient to death—
even death on a cross!

PHILIPPIANS 2:6–8

"A kenotic Christ!" critics of *The Shack* have exclaimed with horror. So, what's the problem? What are they talking about?

The term *kenosis* comes from a classic text in Philippians 2:7. The Greek verb *kenoō* is translated "made himself nothing" by the NIV and "emptied himself" by the NRSV. The term's literal meaning is "empty or pour out," but the metaphorical meaning is "humbled." *Kenosis* or *kenotic* is Paul's language for the intentional self-humiliation of the Son. The one who existed in the form of God became, through incarnation, one who existed in the form of a human being (servant).

What does it mean for the Son to humble himself or empty himself by becoming a human bound over to death? There are many theories as to how this actually happens and what happens. Since the Council of Chalcedon in 451 AD, orthodox Christology has maintained that the Son became human while remaining divine, and at the same time the two natures are distinct and unmixed, though united in one person. *The Shack*, I believe, operates within this orthodox frame. This is clearly difficult for the finite mind to grasp and difficult to portray in a piece of art.

Where I think *The Shack* serves us well is in some of its orthodox but "kenotic" Christology. While it seems clear to me that Young does not suggest a full-blown kenotic theory that denies the deity of Jesus in the flesh (all three do answer "I am" to the question "Which one is God?"), I am not particularly interested in attempting to specify a historical categorization of Young's Christology. Instead, my interest is pastoral rather than historic. My interest is a specific point, which has significant pastoral implications.

Here are some particularly important concepts from *The Shack* for my purpose.

- Jesus lived within the creaturely constraints of humanity and never did anything simply by tapping into a divine nature.
- Jesus was totally dependent, as a human being, upon the Father, and he did not exercise independent power.
- What Jesus sees, he sees through human eyes; he does not have a transcendent vantage point.
- Jesus chose to live as a human, fully immersed in creaturehood, and this choice was driven by his love for humanity.

As I live in my shack, these motifs illuminate something very important to me. Jesus teaches me how to live and be comfortable in my own skin. He became flesh, lived in his own skin, maintained his identity as God's beloved, and loved other people out of that identity. This is how I want to live as well. Jesus apprentices us in how to live a fully authentic human life.

Jesus did not draw on his divinity to get himself out of messes. He did not even perform miracles by an independent exercise of divine power. Rather, he cast out demons *by the Spirit* with whom he had been anointed at his baptism (Matt. 12:28). The Spirit empowered him for the ministry of liberation—freeing the captives, healing the sick, and preaching good news to the poor.

He lived in his own skin—human skin. Human skin, then, is not evil or bad. The incarnation, like God's pronouncement that creation is "very good" (Gen. 1:31), sanctifies materiality. It sanctifies flesh and bone. The flesh—our bodies—are good.

Living in his own skin, Jesus saw the world through human eyes. This is something the Son chose to do—it is a conscious, self-limiting act. He grew in wisdom; he learned obedience. He lived with the limitations of human skin. He lived a "dependent life"—that is, a life wholly dependent upon his Father and the empowering Spirit—to fulfill his mission in the world. He was not an autonomous God in the flesh or an independent agent. Rather, the divine Word (*Logos*) surrendered his power by self-limitation for the purpose of experiencing the cosmos as a "limited" human being, just like the rest of us.

In this way he was tempted just like we are, yet without sin (Heb. 4:15). He lived an authentic human life, which included trials, tribulations, and temptations. He was not only true human (everything humanity was supposed to be as the image of God), but truly (authentically) human.

This is the root of the Son's empathy with humanity. He truly knows what is like to be hungry and thirsty, to be fatigued and suffer pain, to be tempted and to pray as a dependent human being, and to suffer shame and death on a cross. The Son is empathetic because he became like us in every way; he lived in his own skin—a reality he shared with us. Jesus even drops the pancake batter in the cabin kitchen, just as Mack did on the morning Missy disappeared—a subtle, but poignant stroke by Young.

This is one of my comforts, one of my anchors in the storms of life. The empathy of God through Jesus means God understands my suffering and humanity; God has experienced humanity. God knows what it is like—God does not simply know about it, but God has experienced the human condition as an insider. In addition, Papa also has the stigmata—wounds he received through Jesus. The Triune God understands the human condition and predicament.

Though these points are extremely important, the more basic point—and one stressed in *The Shack*—is the *intimacy* God shares with humanity through the union of divine and human in Jesus. We were designed for this union; we were created for communion with God.

The incarnation is the ultimate expression of the divine intent to commune with humanity. The incarnation is an act of *intimacy*. God unites with us—not simply in some moral or ideological vision, but in reality, in the flesh, in our finitude. When God became flesh, he became intimately empathetic. God truly shared himself with us and took our pain up into his own life—but not just our pain, our humanity itself. God became intimate in the most literal and fundamental way possible—he really and personally united the divine and the human.

We are thereby one with God on many levels and in many ways. Just as the Father, Son, and Spirit mutually indwell each other, humanity is included in that communion so that we dwell within the divine communion ourselves. We participate in the *perichoretic* dance! We have not become little gods in any kind of ontological sense, of course, but we do share in the communion of the Triune God. We mutually indwell the divine as the divine dwells in us—we are in them and they are in us. It is an intimacy beyond our imagination, and it is yet to be fully experienced, though we taste it even now.

The picture *The Shack* offers us portrays Jesus as still human but still intimate with the Father and the Spirit—and yet also intimate with us, even now . . . still! When he ascended, he did not divest himself of his humanity. Quite the contrary, he remains the One in whom the divine and human are united, the mediator who as both divine and human reconciles God and humanity. Jesus remains human . . . and will forever remain so.

When I suggest that the Son of God is eternally human—forever our brother, forever our high priest—I sometimes get some surprised looks from people. Many seem to think that upon his return to heaven, the Son of God shed his humanity and returned to his previous existence as simply and solely God. Some apparently think the Son is no longer Jesus—that is, he is no longer human or that at least he will not be human forever.

But the union of the divine and human in the one person—Jesus, the Son of God—is an eternal reality. The Word (John 1:1, 14) gave up an exclusive existence as God to also become human (to add a human nature) and human he will remain. His humanity is now as much a part of his identity as his divinity. The Word did not cease to be God to become human, but neither did the Word put on humanity as a temporary cloak. The Son became human, still is human, and will eternally remain so.

This inspires awe. It is the wonder of the Son's incarnational humiliation. His incarnation was not simply for thirty-three years but was eternal in nature. His humility has an eternal quality. He became human to remain human for the sake of restoring humanity and living eternally as a brother with other humans. How awesome is that?!

Perhaps this is what Papa is talking about when she said to Mack, "One day you folk will understand what he gave up. There are just no words" (193). This is the love of God—Father, Son, and Spirit. This is the sacrifice of God for our sakes. This is the mystery of redemption (1 Tim. 3:16).

Then again, perhaps we will never understand, but we will have an eternity to explore the wonder of what the Son gave up for us and how the Triune God took humanity up into their own life and communion. What a wonder it will be!

Wounded people need to hear that someone truly loves them that much. They feel unloved and unlovable, and the incarnation testifies to the love of God. God loved us so much that God became human for our sakes. The Word emptied himself in order to fill us up. The Word became poor that we might become rich.

Was it worth the price? "Absolutely!" Jesus says to Mack, "And I would have done it even if it were *only* for you!" (105). These words of Jesus, however, are not for Mack alone. They speak to you and me. We are worth that much to God. You and I are important, worthy of love. We are worth it!

CHAPTER 21

God and Evil:
Can God Be Justified?

*Oh, the depths of the riches of the wisdom and
knowledge of God!
How unsearchable his judgments,
and his paths beyond tracing out!
"Who has known the mind of the Lord?
Or who has been his counselor?"*

ROMANS 11:33–34

The death of a child, especially the brutal murder of
Missy, raises passionate questions about God's handling of the
world. Mack's last comment to the Triune God around the
breakfast table on that first morning was something all of us
have thought at one time or another: "I just can't imagine any
final outcome that would justify all this" (129).

145

There it is. Bold. In God's face. It is almost a gauntlet challenging God's own imagination, God's own resources—God's wisdom and knowledge. Can anything justify the evil present in the world?

This is the problem of theodicy—that is, the justification of God. Why does God create a world in which evil is so pervasive, strong, and unruly? Why does he give evil this space to grow? When a cyclone kills over one hundred thirty thousand in Myanmar, an earthquake snuffs out the lives of eighty thousand more in China, children are murdered at their school by a lone gunman, and ISIS-like terrorism fills the earth, I have little interest in defending or justifying God.

When my son dies of a genetic disorder after I watch him slowly degenerate over ten years, and I learn of the tragic death of a friend's son (John Robert Dobbs)—both dying on the same date, May 21—I have little interest in defending or justifying God.

How could I possibly defend any of that? I suppose I could remove God from responsibility by disconnecting him from his creation, but I would then still have a God who decided to be a Deist. That's no comfort—it renders God malevolent or at least disinterested. Or I could argue God has so limited God's own self that God becomes impotent (even uncertain) in the face of evil, especially particular evils over which the people of God have prayed. But that cuts the heart out of prayer in so many ways and ultimately is another way to protect God from getting his hands dirty. I prefer to say God is involved and decides to permit (even cause—though I would have no way of knowing which is the case in any particular circumstance) suffering. I would prefer to hold God responsible for the world God created and how the world proceeds.

I'm tired of defending God. Does God really need my feeble, finite, and fallible defensive arguments? Perhaps some need to hear a defense—maybe it would help, but I also know it is woefully inadequate at many levels. God does not need my defense so much as God needs to encounter people in their crises. My arguments will not make the difference; only God's presence will.

I know the fancy theodicies, and I have attempted them myself. Young utilizes a few of them. A freewill theodicy roots evil in the free choices of human beings, but this does not help me with earthquakes, genetics, and cyclones. It certainly does not explain why God does not answer passionate, righteous prayers with compassionate protection from such. Soul-making theodicies say God permits evil to develop our character, but this does not explain the quantity and quality of suffering in the world. Suffering sometimes breaks souls rather than making them. There are other theodicies and combinations, but I find them all pastorally inadequate and rationally unsatisfying.

At the same time, I am not the measure of the universe, and God cannot fit inside my brain. I must rest in the truth that the reality of suffering is something beyond my rational abilities to justify. But that does not mean God does not have reasons. It only means I don't know them, and human finitude, fallibility, and egos are too limiting to know them or even understand them.

My rationalizations have all shipwrecked on the rocks of experience in a hurting and painful world. The way I most often approach God in the midst of suffering is now *protest*, a form of lament.

Does God have a good reason for the pervasive and seemingly gratuitous nature of suffering in the world? I hope God does—I even believe God does, but I don't know what the reasons are, nor do I know anyone who does. My hope is not the conclusion of a well-reasoned, solid inductive/deductive argument. It is rather the desperate cry of the sufferer who trusts that the Creator has good intentions and purposes for the creation. I believe there is a Grand Purpose that overcomes the Great Sadness, and this is the story the Bible tells.

Lament is not exactly a theodicy, but it is my response to suffering. It contains my complaint that God is not doing more (Ps. 74:11), my questions about "how long?" (Ps. 13:1), my demand to have my "Why?" questions answered (Ps. 44:24), and my disillusionment with God's handling of the world (Job 21, 23–24). It is what I feel; it is my only "rational" response to suffering.

I realize I am a lowly creature whose limitations should relativize my protest (as when God came to Job), though this does not minimize it. On the contrary, God commended Job's honesty and his willingness to speak "right" to God (42:7–12).

Learning from Job and the psalmists, I continue to lament—I continue because I have divine permission to do so! Of all people, I must be honest with God, right? I recognize my feeble laments cannot grasp the transcendent glory of the One who created the world, and I realize that, were God to speak, God would say to me something like what Job heard. But until God speaks, until God comforts, until God transforms the world, I will continue to speak, lament, and protest.

But that response is itself insufficient. I protest, but I must also act.

As one who believes the story of Jesus, I trust that God intends to redeem, heal, and renew this world. As a disciple of Jesus, I am committed to imitate his compassion for the hurting, to participate in the healing, and to sacrifice for redemption. I am, however, at this point an impatient disciple.

Does this mean that there are no comforting "words" for the sufferer? No, I think the story itself is a comfort; we have a story to tell, but we must tell it without rationalizing or minimizing creation's pain. We have a story to tell about God, Israel, and Jesus.

God loves us despite the seeming evidence to the contrary. God listens to our protests despite our anger and disillusionment. God empathizes with our suffering through the incarnation despite our sense that no one has suffered like we have. God reigns over his world despite the seeming chaos and senseless evil. God will defeat suffering and renew his creation despite its current tragic condition. The story carries hope in its bosom, and we grieve with hope

Mack could not envision anything that could justify all the evil in the world. This is something Mack says before he sits on the judgment seat before Sophia, but it is a function of the judgment seat to decide what would justify evil and what would not. If humans can't imagine it, then it can't be possible, right? And that is the crux of the problem—human imagination has become the norm rather than trusting God's wisdom and knowledge that are beyond searching out, plotting, or understanding.

Human imagination or trust in divine wisdom? Which shall we choose? The former, as a criterion, excludes the latter. The latter is patient with the former's limitations.

But trust is the fundamental problem. At the root of distrust is the suspicion, as Papa tells Mack, "that you don't think that I am good." We humans tend to trust our own imagination (or rationality) more than we trust God's goodness. We doubt everything is "covered by [God's] goodness." (128).

In one of the most powerful scenes in *The Shack*, Papa acknowledges that she could "have prevented what happened to Missy." Papa chose to not intervene even though she could have done so (224). Only love enables Mack to trust God with that decision.

We can't imagine what could possibly justify evil. But, at one level, that is the wrong question. *God's purpose is not to justify it, but to redeem it.*

My favorite scene in Mel Gibson's *The Passion of Christ* is when Jesus, carrying the cross, falls to his knees under its weight. His mother runs to him, and their eyes lock. With blood streaming down his cheeks and holding the symbol of Roman power and violence, Jesus says, "Behold, Mother, I make all things new." In the depths of this suffering—in the depths of all suffering—is the seed of redemptive love, though it is invisible to us and everything we see with our eyes tells us otherwise. Nevertheless, in the midst of the suffering—paradigmatically at the cross—God is at work to renew all things.

This is the promise of God—a new creation, new heavens and a new earth in a new Jerusalem. There, the old order will pass away and the voice of God will declare, "I am making everything new" (Rev. 21:5).

A day is coming when there will be "no more curse" (Rev. 22:3). There will be no more darkness—the glory of God will fill the earth with light. There will be no more violence—the nations will receive healing and walk by its light. There will be no more death, mourning, or tears—the Tree of Life and the Water of Life will nourish the people of God forever.

That renewal, however, is not simply future but is already present. Hope saves us even now. As the Father pours out divine love into our hearts by the Spirit, includes us in the Triune fellowship at the breakfast table, and walks with us in our suffering, we experience the joy of relationship, the peace of love, and the hope of renewal.

Mack discovered it when he learned to trust. We will too.

CHAPTER 22

Weaving a Tapestry of Love: Divine Providence

*And we know that in all things God works
for the good of those who love him, who have been
called according to his purpose.*

ROMANS 8:28

The Shack recognizes the pervasive, rooted, and intensive presence of evil in the world. The source of this evil, according to the parable, is ultimately human freedom, as humanity chose autonomy rather than dependence upon God. We chose to create our own story rather than participate in God's Grand Purpose. And when we chose this path, we dragged the whole creation into the muck with us.

The Triune God respects this freedom since it is God's own design, and God has "never taken control" of human choices and "forced" humanity "to do anything" (147).

But this does not render God powerless. Through much of the dialogue between Mack and God, there is a wondrous sense that God is neither hamstrung nor thwarted by the freedom Papa gives humanity. God sometimes works around it, sometimes through it, and sometimes against it, but at all times God pursues divine purposes, and those purposes will not be frustrated. God uses human freedom as part of the divine purposes, and God knows how to connect the dots.

But, Mack quietly voiced at the breakfast table, "What is the value in a little girl being murdered by some twisted deviant? You may not cause those things," Mack continued, "but you certainly don't stop them" (127).

God has his purposes—there are reasons he does not hinder every evil choice, but those reasons are as big as the cosmos itself and as specific as the story of every individual person. The web of relationship is much too complex for human wisdom, because every person is the center of a story unknown by others.

Everyone's story connects to another story, and those connections reverberate throughout the present world and down through history. The Grand Story is much too complex for limited minds such as ours, and yet in the midst of that complexity God pursues the Grand Purpose, while at the same time making every human story the focus of divine attention. In this sense God permits suffering and evil, like the death of Missy, for reasons no one could begin to understand in the present. The world and the story of divine purpose within it are much too complex, too intricate, to comprehend. Even if God did explain it to us, it is more than we could grasp. It would be like a physicist explaining quantum mechanics to a three-year-old.

The Grand Story unfolds the Grand Purpose. God intends to share with humanity the Triune fellowship itself. God created humanity to join their "circle of love." And, Papa lovingly assures Mack at the breakfast table, "Everything that has taken place is occurring exactly according to this purpose, without violating choice or will," even though that was beyond Mack's imagination (127).

Is everything as it is supposed to be? Perhaps not, but everything that happens serves the Grand Purpose of God within the Grand Story God is authoring. According to Papa, God's sovereign purposes are greater than any human choice, and God moves within the world for the sake of the Grand Purpose, which will yield in the lives of people an unimaginable result they are not able to see at the moment.

The Grand Purpose ultimately overcomes the Great Sadness. God does not, according to *The Shack*, "orchestrate the tragedies" or cause them, but "where there is suffering you will find grace in many facets and colors" (185).

Where was God when Missy was kidnapped? Where was the grace in that? At one level, the divine purpose is much too complicated to unpack, but at another level, the grace of God was present to eyes that could see and ears that could hear . . . even in the dark moment of Missy's kidnapping.

Do you remember Jesse and Sarah from the campground? They are the presence of Jesus and the Holy Spirit around the fire the night prior to Missy's abduction. Sarah is Sarayu, and

Jesse is another name for Jesus (as Jesus tells Mack in the cabin). This is the couple Mack immediately liked, who loved on his children, with whom Mack found himself in an intimate but uncomfortable relationship. God was with Mack that morning when Missy went missing—Jesse and Sarah were with him. And when Nan arrived, Sarah wept with and interceded for her—the role of the Holy Spirit in our lives. Jesse hugged Mack and told him they would meet again.

God's gracious moments are present even in the darkness. Though sometimes disguised, they are present. The hurt blinds us so easily and our wounds bind us so tightly that the grace is hidden from our sight.

The more our wounds heal through increasing intimacy with God and with others, the more we are able to see the wounds as part of the process. The journey, in the judgment of *The Shack*, is worth it just as Jesus's own journey through his Great Sadness was worth it. The Grand Purpose within the Grand Story draws us into intimacy—into the "circle of love"—which heals and redeems.

God, as Romans 8:28 promises, is at work in everything for good. But this good is God's Grand Purpose, which is to conform us to the image of the Son. This is the good God has in mind and not the sort of things we materialistic, self-serving humans usually have defined as happiness. In God's Grand Purpose, happiness is intimacy with God and not, for example, the accumulation of stuff or even—dare we say it?—the health of our children.

The providential work of God in our lives through our sadnesses, our tragedies, our wounds, even our sins, draws us deeper into God's own life. God takes our chaos and "weaves a magnificent tapestry" (179). Progressively, though imperfectly, wounded people can learn to embrace the way that even the dark shades of the tapestry become part of a wondrous story.

The Grand Purpose of God will give meaning even to the Great Sadness.

The Heart of
SPIRITUAL
Recovery

CHAPTER 23

"I Will Change Your Name"

When you feel forsaken or rejected,
when you feel like a failure or a piece of dirt,
when you feel inadequate or deficient,
when you feel unloved or unchosen,
hear the word of the Lord through Isaiah the prophet:

You will be called by a new name
that the mouth of the LORD will bestow . . .
No longer will they call you Deserted,
or name your land Desolate.
But you will be called Hephzibah ["my delight"],
and your land Beulah ["married"];
for the Lord will take delight in you,
and your land will be married.
. . . as a bridegroom rejoices over his bride,
so will your God rejoice over you.

ISAIAH 62:2B, 4, 5B

Isaiah's message is for postexilic Israel (56–66). The people had returned from exile only to find themselves still oppressed, poor, and seemingly abandoned to their fate. They lived under heavy Persian taxation and were harassed by regional provinces. Jerusalem's walls were in ruins. Famine and poverty were rampant. The return did not meet expectations; it was not all that it was cracked up to be. Where was the glory of the restoration, the return to the land of promise? The promises of God had seemed to fail. Israel had been deserted and the land was desolate; Israel was rejected and ruined. The people of God were losing hope; they felt unchosen.

Isaiah 56–59 outlined Judah's sins, but Isaiah 60–62 proclaims a message of grace and salvation. Isaiah 62:1–5 is the climax of that message. God will not give up on Israel. God has chosen Jerusalem; it belongs to God. God will not relent. God's love endures forever. God will change Jerusalem's name, just as with Abram (to Abraham), Sarai (to Sarah), and Jacob (to Israel) long ago.

Names Matter

God's names reveal the divine character. *Yahweh-Yireh* is the Lord who Provides (Gen. 22:14). *Yahweh-Shalom* is the Lord of Wholeness (Judg. 6:24). *Yahweh-Mekedesh* is the Lord who Sanctifies (Ezek. 37:28). The name Yahweh means "the one who is" or "I am that I am." The name of God matters as it defines God, and our names matter too because they define us.

What Others Call Us Matters

They matter because in our wounded condition we absorb those names within our hearts. "Sticks and stones may break my bones, but names will never hurt me" is a lie. When, as preadolescents, we were labeled "different" or "weird," some of us internalized a life-long stigma in our own minds. Such language and experiences shaped our core beliefs. When we were constantly picked last on the playground, we were named "unchosen." When a parent abandoned us, we were named "unworthy." When we were abused, we were named "worthless."

What We Call Ourselves Matters

If, at our core, we call ourselves worthless," "unloved," or "pathetic," it will shape how we relate to people. It will shape the nature of our marriages, our parenting, and our relationships. It will shape our churches. Indeed, self-righteousness within churches is often more a matter of maintaining a self-image and ignoring the truth about oneself than it is about the welcoming, forgiving holiness of God.

What God Calls Us Truly Matters

And it matters more than our own inadequate and inaccurate views of ourselves do. How we hear God—the sieve through which we filter God's word to us—often twists God's naming. Though intellectually we may hear God say "beloved," if our core is filled with shame, hurt, pain, wounds, and abandonment and if our image of God has been shaped by pictures of Zeus holding lightning bolts, eager to inflict retribution, what we hear is not "beloved" but "loathed." Since we believe—at our core or gut—that we are not worth loving, we cannot believe that God could actually love us in the midst of our shame, abandonment, and sin.

How Do I Name Myself?

Only recently have I recognized with any depth the significance of other's names for us and our names for ourselves. I have discovered that at my core—in my own self-image—I had lived with some names that have negatively impacted me. Whether self-generated, imposed by others, or impressed by circumstances, these names nearly destroyed me in 2008. Here are a few of my "old" names for myself.

Forsaken

I felt this intensely when Sheila died in 1980 after only two years and eleven months of marriage. I felt it again when Joshua was diagnosed with a terminal genetic defect and then died at the age of sixteen in 2001.

Why, God, have you forsaken me? Will you forsake me forever? Why are you picking on me? Is there something wrong with me? Why do you rip away my joy and fill my heart with sorrow?

Failure

I have felt this most deeply since my divorce. I failed at the most important relationship in my life.

During that trauma, I was disillusioned, confused, and deeply hurt. I now own much more of the causes of that divorce than I did in 2001, but this only increases my sense of failure. The name, seemingly, only gets more appropriate with time and fuller self-understanding.

Deficient

One of my early core beliefs is "I am not enough." Consequently, emotionally, I have sought approval, and the most effective mode for that was through work. Approval-seeking became an addiction.

I am a workaholic. I stuffed myself with addictive behavior in order to feel good about myself, to gain approval and connect with others. But ultimately, it was an empty feeling. Whatever approval I received was never enough; I always needed more and was envious when others received acclaim. And I needed more because at my core—somehow, someway—I had been named "Deficient."

What is your name? How have you been named? What have you felt in your gut and believed at your core that has shaped how you see yourself, others, and God?

I am only beginning to understand the names I have worn. But I know there is something better. God has named me. Those are the names I want to internalize. I want to see myself and others through the lens of God's naming.

God Changes Names

Israel and I have chewed some of the same dirt. Forsaken . . . Rejected . . . Desolate. Indeed, we have all worn these names in one form or another. But there is good news—there is gospel. God changes names, and only God can truly do so. To try to change my own name is an illusion, futile, and another attempt to fill what is lacking by my own efforts. God must name me and, when God does name me, God actualizes it—God makes it a reality!

Isaiah provides a startling image for us by which we enter this story emotionally as well as intellectually. Yahweh's new name for Israel is "My delight is in her"—the one in whom God delights. God loves her, enjoys being with her, and yearns for her presence. Yahweh's name for Israel is "Married"—God unites with Israel for the sake of intimacy; God wants to know this bride. Yahweh rejoices over Israel just as a bridegroom rejoices over his bride—God's joy surpasses a wedding celebration. God joins in the wedding dance and surrounds Israel with love.

This is how God feels. This is the truth about God's people. "I will rejoice over you," declares Yahweh. The King of the cosmos does not sit on his throne without emotional engagement with the creation. Quite the contrary, God chooses a bride, delights in her, dresses her in a bridal gown, and celebrates her with dancing and festivity.

This is how God feels about us. Our past, self-styled names are false names—they are no longer true, if they ever were. We have new names—names bestowed by God. No longer are we "Forsaken," but we are "Chosen." No longer are we "Failure," but we are "Married." No longer are we "Deficient," but we are "Blessed"! Though God knows the depths of our hearts (which are not always pretty), the Father loves us just as the Father loves the Son (John 17:23).

God's word to each of us, as it was to Jesus, is, "You are beloved; you are the one in whom I delight." God welcomes us, dresses us in festive robes, spreads a table of the best food and the finest wines, and spends the evening dancing with the bride. God wants us and stands in applause as we wear the names given to us: Chosen, Beloved, Married, and Blessed.

The lyrics of D. J. Butler's "I Will Change Your Name" speak the essence of this text; hear them, believe them. It is the word of God through Isaiah to each of us.

I will change your name
You shall no longer be called
Wounded, outcast, lonely or afraid.

I will change your name
Your new name shall be
Confidence, joyfulness, overcoming one
Faithfulness, friend of God
One who seeks My face.

CHAPTER 24

You Are Loved!

[You] have loved them even as you have loved me.

JOHN 17:23

One Wednesday evening in November of 2008, I was blessed to hear Terry Smith teach. Terry was one of the ministers of the Woodmont Hills Family of God in Nashville at that time, and he is one of God's precious messengers who have ministered to me in my brokenness and helped me in my own spiritual recovery.

Terry stressed how we each are beloved by God. That is sometimes difficult to believe. One close friend confided in me that he, too, finds it difficult. But he can approach it through something like this: John 3:16 says that God loves the world—inclusive of all the people who have committed even the most atrocious evils, and the world includes him—and me. God loves us even when we don't love ourselves or others. John 3:16 includes me.

But from that particular evening when Terry spoke, one line has stuck with me in a special way. It was a text Terry emphasized. It is a line from John 17 that I had read many times and had even translated from the original language on multiple occasions, but that night, I experienced it in a new way. I believe it began to sink deep into my heart. I want it to sink even deeper.

In my thinking and teaching about John 17, I have regularly underscored the love the Father and the Son have for each other and how God seeks to draw us into the circle of their love, just as I have stressed so far in this short book. The Father and Son intend for us to experience the love they share. As John 17:26 states, we are designed (created for the purpose!) to know (experience and enjoy!) the love the Father has for the Son. We are created to dwell in the love the Father and Son share with each other.

But Terry stressed a different line in this prayer—different even from the laudable and traditional emphasis on unity from verses 20–21 that has characterized most lessons I have heard from this chapter.

Terry stressed a single declarative statement in verse 23. Jesus says to the Father, "*You have loved them even as you have loved me.*"

Wow! Let that sink in. Dwell on it for a moment. Take some time to let that ping throughout the corners of your brain, and your heart, and your gut.

I had read it before; many times—many, many times. I had read it more times than I could possibly remember and even translated it from the original Greek on multiple occasions. For the first time perhaps, that night, I really felt it in my gut.

The Father loves the disciples just as he loves Jesus. Yes, the disciples. The tax collector? The sinful, cursing, impetuous fisherman sarcastically (perhaps) named "the rock"? The Zealot—the political agitator? Judas the betrayer—no, the betrayers!? They all betrayed him; they all ran eventually. They would all hide.

The Father loves the disciples just as he loves Jesus. The Father loves screw-ups (like Mack, like me). The Father loves those who don't understand him. God loves those who betray the Son. God loves those who live in fear rather than faith. The Father loves them in their brokenness, their humanity, their finitude, even in their sin.

The Father loves the disciples just as the Father loves Jesus. No more, no less. God is love, and the love between the Father and the Son is the love with which the Father loves the disciples. The disciples are loved, even when they don't feel loved and know they are loved.

The Father loves me just as he loves Jesus. Can it really be true? Surely not! I understand why the Father loves the Son. Jesus was the perfect Son! Obedient. Transparent. Loving. Submissive. Jesus was everything the Father could ask for in a son.

However, it is exactly this rationale that makes it so difficult for me to believe the Father loves me. Somehow and in some way, my heart believes God only loves those who are worthy of love, deserve love, or are the perfect children.

I have screwed up so many times. I am broken. I know myself too well. How can God love me when my shack is so broken, dirty, and seemingly irreparable?

But the Father knows me, too. And the Father loves me just the same . . . even as the Father loves the Son. Because God loves me, I am worthy of love! God's love renders me worthy; it is not my worth that demands God's love. The love of God is a gift; it is not something earned. And God gives it because God is love.

The Father loves me just as the Father loves Jesus. What a wondrous thought; what a powerful, transforming truth! This is the truth I need to believe; this is the truth that needs to sink deep within me. This is the truth that should shape my heart, ground my security, and produce my joy. This love is what is really real; it is the truth of the gospel. It is the truth that is the foundation of a redeemed cosmos. My Father loves me just like Jesus.

It is not really a new truth, of course. But it entered my heart and gut in a new way that evening. It is the kind of newness that I need every day. I need to hear that truth anew every day and know deep within me that the mercies of God are new every morning.

With this truth, I can crawl into my Father's lap, trust in the Father's care, and feel the Father's loving arms enwrap me. Thank you, Father.

Thank you, Jesus, for demonstrating that love at the Cross.

Thank you, Holy Spirit, for pouring that love into my heart.

CHAPTER 25

Faith Instead of Fear: Learning to Trust God

*They will have no fear of bad news;
their hearts are steadfast, trusting in the LORD.*

PSALM 112:7

Our God is often too small, and our pride too big.

Our pride generates either folly or fear. Our pride may so blind us that we live arrogantly, self-righteously, and judgmentally—but we are so prideful that we don't even see our faults. This is the definition of folly.

For others, pride generates fear because we want control but we recognize that we do not have control. We think that if we can control the circumstances of our lives, we can eliminate fear and generate our own serenity. Pride cannot admit we are not in control; pride cannot confess powerlessness.

To confess pride opens the door for trust.

We humans have a tendency to think that God can only do what we can imagine, what we can think up for ourselves. Somehow, we think God is limited by our own imagination. As Papa explained to Mack, "You try to make sense of the world in which you live based on a very small and incomplete picture of reality." And even that picture is filtered through the lens of "hurt, pain, self-centeredness, and power."

Ultimately, this creates fear, as we seek to manipulate and control the world around us. But we soon discover that we are unable to control it or even make sense of it. That generates more fear. The more we fear, the more we want to control, and the more we recognize our powerlessness, the more we want to control. This degenerative cycle produces isolation, distrust, and/or unbelief.

Our pain, our brokenness, and our wounded souls confirm our powerlessness, and fear dominates as we wait for the proverbial "next shoe to drop." We live by fear rather than by trust; we live by sight rather than by faith.

To confess fear opens the door for faith.

How do we learn to trust when we live with so much fear?

On the one hand, learning to trust is *unlearning* self-reliance; learning to trust is *learning* dependence. Our self-reliance is ingrained, but this very self-reliance (pride) is the soil in which fear is planted. Since fear is selfish and self-centered, we unlearn fear through depending on another.

It is the strange nature of the world where the very hurts and pains that generate fear are the tools God uses to help us unlearn our self-reliance.

On the other hand, learning to trust is a proactive process. Like taking our first steps as a baby, we learn to walk surrounded by the love of parents and encouragers. We step out—we put our foot forward—in faith. We stumble and we sometimes fall, but we keep walking till we learn to run.

Learning to trust is relational rather than cognitive. It is not about how much we know but about how much we connect. It is not so much about mechanics (a kind of "how to trust" manual) as it is about intimacy.

Intimacy is something we learn through active connection with others. While *The Shack* has sometimes been criticized for its neglect of community (some see a negative view of "church" in the book), Young stresses the importance of relationships. Intimacy is about relationships rather than institutions, about connectedness rather than structures. Intimacy can certainly happen within structures or institutions (or within "church"), but intimacy does not happen because of them. Intimacy is truly being present with another—transparent and open. That cannot be structured or institutionalized.

This is what Mack learned over the weekend—what Paul Young learned through ten years of recovery. Learning to trust God means being with God—openly, honestly, and intentionally. Mack learned how to be intimate by participating in the intimacy of the Father, Son, and Spirit. He learned to trust God by being with God.

That is well and good for a parable, but what does it mean for me? I have not yet had a vision like Mack. Rightly or wrongly, I don't expect one. But what I do have is the historic practices of believers through the ages who have experienced God through intentional spiritual habits. Through solitude, silence, simplicity of life, prayer, meditation, Scripture reading, and so on, they have encountered God. They have learned to be with God, to rest upon God's breast, and to trust God.

My good friend Terry Smith practices being with God every morning. He sits in his morning meditation chair and with sanctified imagination envisions the Triune God as sitting with him. He addresses the Father, then the Son, and then the Spirit. He reads the word of God. He listens. He speaks. He enjoys. He begins his day with an intimate experience of God. I have often followed his example in recent years.

This was Mack's experience. Rising from his bed, he went to the breakfast table where he sat with God—Papa, Jesus, and Sarayu. He talked. He listened. He wept. He questioned. And he learned to trust.

We cannot learn to trust if we are never with God. If we never intentionally seek God's presence or seek the intimacy of the Triune God, we continue to live in fear rather than faith.

But this is difficult for many people. It has often been difficult for me. When I am so shut down emotionally in my relationships with others, how can I ever experience or know that it means or feels like to be intimate with God? Intimacy with others teaches us how to be intimate with God or at least teaches us what intimacy is.

This is why we need community. We need "church"—not because of the institution, structures, or buildings. We need community (church) because we learn intimacy by being with others. This is one reason 12-step or AA meetings (in whatever form they come) are so powerful. Their members form community, practice intimacy, as they share their lives and develop their ability to trust.

Church has often failed miserably at this, but most often because we have misidentified "church" with its institutional trappings. When we think of church as a community of fellow-believers—indeed, fellow-sinners—who seek intimacy with God, perhaps we can learn to walk with each other in grace, forgiveness, and accountability. We can then become authentic "church."

And when church comes together as a whole (like on a Sunday morning for most traditions), it comes together to listen to God, to talk with God, to eat and drink with God at Jesus's table, and to enjoy God. It comes *together*—yes, as a community—to share the Triune intimacy *together*. It comes to sit at the table with the Triune God.

But we cannot develop intimacy with others simply through large communal experiences like Sunday morning assemblies. We truly learn intimacy in small settings where we share our hearts, our lives, and our secrets.

When we let other people into our shacks, when we let them see who we really are, what we really believe and value, then we experience intimacy. And when we experience authentic intimacy, then we know what love is.

When I have risked opening my shack up to other people in intimate settings—and it is a risk, because we are uncertain how they will react, what they will say, or what they will do—I have experienced acceptance, forgiveness, and love in my church community.

When we experience love, we can learn to trust as others love and trust us. "Trust," Papa told Mack, "is the fruit or a relationship in which you know you are loved" (128). When we are loved, we can trust. And the more we receive and give love, the less room there is for fear, and the ability to give and receive love grows. Fear dissipates as love increases; there is no room for fear when the heart is filled with love.

God, community, and intimate friends can repair our broken "trust-ers." Many people don't know how to trust or even what it feels like to trust another person. They do not trust because they don't feel loved. We trust when we know we are loved.

Living in an accepting, welcoming, and open community; living with close and intimate friends; and intentionally seeking God through solitude and silence, we learn to trust again because we know we are loved.

We turn fears into trust when we turn cares into prayers. And we pray because we know we are loved.

When our God is too small and our pride is too big, fear dominates. But when we confess God as big (the Creator, Lover, and Redeemer) and ourselves as small (creature, loved, and sinner), trust grows in our hearts.

God is big and we are small. Therefore, we trust.

CHAPTER 26

The Circle of Love: Turning Mourning into Dancing

You turned my wailing into joyful dancing;
you removed sackcloth and clothed me with joy.

PSALM 30:11

The beginning and end of *The Shack* stand in radical contrast. At the beginning of the story, Mack's appearance was brooding, dark, and disturbing, but at the end, he is vibrant, loving, and accepting. In the beginning, his relationship with God was shallow, but after a weekend at the shack it has gone "deep." Mack's weekend encounter with God at the shack was transformative.

Some have judged the parable too rosy in its ending, too facile, too ideal. Some have almost ridiculed the idea that a weekender with God could solve all one's problems. While the story is not that artificial, we should remember that this weekend is actually a summary of Young's ten-year journey into spiritual recovery.

His mourning was not turned into dancing over a weekend but through a decade-long journey of reconciliation with wife and family, prolonged therapy, and focused spiritual discipline. The weekender in *The Shack* may seem glib or fanciful, but it is actually a summary of ten years of spiritual recovery. The parable telescopes ten years into three days.

The point is this: God does turn mourning into dancing. God can change us; God can transform us. God can make light shine in the darkness. God can change our clothes.

It does not seem possible, however, when we are mourning. It can seem hopeless. We cannot imagine we will ever see happiness again, even when we fool ourselves into believing better days are coming.

Mourning comes from at least two sources. Mourning descends on us because the Great Sadness in our lives blinds us to the vibrant colors of life. The Great Sadness breaks our "trust-ers" because we feel unloved. The tragedies and traumas of our wounded lives strip us of the ability to trust because we believe that our anguished soul means we are unloved and perhaps even unlovable.

Mourning also descends on us because we feel like miserable failures who disappoint others, ourselves, and even God. We are often people who live by rules rather than living in relationships. We judge our worth on our ability to live by the rules, to be successful, to make something of ourselves, to gain the approval of others, or to please others. We get our value from performance rather than love. Indeed, we tend to think we make ourselves lovable when we perform well.

Religion addicts are particularly adept at such thinking, as are others (like workaholics, for example). In our heads we know God loves us despite our performance, but in our gut, we believe our performance is what really counts, and if we don't perform, God would not love us—or at least wouldn't love us as much.

Somehow, in some way, we learned that how well we are doing in life (are our children healthy? how successful is our work? no big tragedies, no big mistakes?) is the judge of how much we are loved. Somehow, someway we learned—in our gut even when our head denied it—that God loves only those who perform well. Our lovability—whether we were worthy of love or not—depended on how well we knew the rules and how well we kept them. And if we keep the rules—if we please God—then life should be rosy, undisturbed by tragedy, and successful.

It is no wonder that we live in fear—we are ultimately afraid God does not really love us. We compensate by studying the rules, living by the rules, and enforcing the rules on others. Rather than helping, we become judgmental, vindictive (at times just downright mean), and miserable people—if not on the outside, on the inside. And the reason is, as Sarayu told Mack, "There is no mercy or grace in rules, not even for one mistake" (204).

The Shack addresses this head-on. *How do wounded people come to believe that God really cares for them?* Young's parable was written to answer that question, and we have come back to it time and again throughout this book. It is the fundamental question that opens the door for relationship, intimacy, and joy. When wounded people come to believe that God deeply loves them, it turns their mourning into dancing.

Mack's weekend with God, when Papa comforted Mackenzie, was about intimacy and community. It was not about rules and performance. Papa wanted Mack to know that performance is not the basis of their relationship. An authentic sense of pleasing God does not arise out of the demands of performance but out of the experience of loving in relationship.

But this is very hard to grasp. If performance is not the key, then why does God love us when God receives no benefit or reward from us? But that God loves us when we have nothing that would complete him or add worth to him—this is, in fact, the very thing that "alleviate[s] any pressure to perform."

God loves us because that is who God is. God—Papa, Jesus, and Sarayu—are a circle of love. They are love; God is love. God loves because of who God is, not because of how well we have performed. We are worthy of love because God has loved us. God created us as the center of the circle of their love.

This is the circle we are invited to join. It is a circle engaged in the joyful dance of love.

I love the visual image of people dancing in a circle whether it is a Greek dance like in the film *My Big Fat Greek Wedding* or a Jewish dance like in *Fiddler on the Roof*. Joined in hand, filled with joy, they circle the center. Those scenes tap into a deep desire to join the dance and feel the joy.

This is the dance of the Triune God. And we—yes, astoundingly, *we*—are the center of that circle. We are the center of God's love and relationship. We are the concern (along with the rest of creation) of God's Grand Purpose. We are loved and celebrated; we are God's delight. We are beloved!

Moreover, we join God in the "circle of relationship." We join the dance. As dancers—as participants—we encircle others who have yet to join. We love them so that they may know that they, too, are the center of God's love, and we invite them to join the dance.

We become not merely passive recipients of God's Grand Purpose, but we become participants in the mission of God to encircle every human being with the love of God so that they, too, may join the dance.

Come, join the dance!

You are invited, beloved, and chosen!

God turns our mourning into dancing!

Chapter Discussion Questions

Introduction—Chapter One

1. How do parables draw us into a story and then sucker-punch us? How does this happen in the Parable of the Prodigal Son (Luke 16), and how does this happen in *The Shack*?

2. What question does *The Shack* address? How does this question reflect your own experience? How does it touch you?

Chapter Two

1. What does *The Shack* represent in the parable and in Young's own life? What is your shack?

2. What are some of the unhealthy ways we hide, neglect, or ignore our shacks?

Chapter Three

1. How do we construct our own shacks? How do the circumstances of life as well as others in our lives shape how our shacks appear?

2. What are some of the experiences that have constructed your shack?

Chapter Four

1. What was your initial response to Madeleine L'Engle's letter to God? How does it resonate with you? In what ways does it not? Does it make sense to you?

2. What do we do with our anger towards God? When have you been angry with God? What did you do with that anger?

Chapter Five

1. Why is opening the door to the shack such an important moment in the parable? Why are we afraid to look inside our shacks and seek God?

2. What is your first memory of God? What image of God dominates your thoughts, fears, and shame? Who is the God behind the door of your shack?

Chapter Six

1. What is your "Great Sadness"? How does it color the different parts of your life?

2. What are some unhealthy ways to experience or respond to your "Great Sadness"?

3. Why are tears so often an embarrassment for us?

Chapter Seven

1. What happens when our "Great Sadness" becomes our identity? How does that happen? Why does it happen?

2. How does trust replace fear so that we are able to endure our "Great Sadness"? What enables trust, even in the midst of a great sadness?

Chapter Eight

1. How does the metaphor of our souls as gardens illuminate God's work in us and our role in that work?

2. How does psychodrama empower us to reconstruct and give new meaning to our traumatic experiences? How does psychodrama function in the life of the church and its assemblies?

3. What experience or moment moves Mack from being stuck in his Great Sadness to being free from it? How do we move from "stuck" to "endurance" when we face our great sadnesses?

Chapter Nine

1. Using your own sanctified imagination, describe what Peter felt when Jesus fixed his eyes on him.

2. What image(s) of God have shaped your experience of God's gaze upon your shack?

Chapter Ten

1. What does it mean to say forgiveness is a gift we give to others and to ourselves?

2. What empowers forgiveness? What hinders forgiveness?

3. What is the difference between forgiveness and reconciliation?

Chapter Eleven

1. In what ways is self-forgiveness a positive and empowering act? How might some view it negatively? Why do some consider it a negative?

2. What is the ground or basis for self-forgiveness? What empowers self-forgiveness?

3. Why is it important to forgive ourselves? What negative consequences result when we do not forgive ourselves?

Chapter Twelve

1. What was your first gut response to the title "Forgiving God"? Why did you feel that way?
2. What does it mean to forgive God? Why does the failure to forgive God result in bitter resentment?

Chapter Thirteen

1. Do you remember a moment when you resented how God had acted or not acted in your life? Describe that feeling. What is at the root of that experience?
2. How do we release our resentment toward God? By what process might we learn to accept the reality in front of us and "forgive God"?

Chapter Fourteen

1. Did Jesus, as a human being, need intimacy? How did he become intimate with others?
2. What is intimacy? Why do we need it? What does it look like?
3. What kinds of intimacy do you have in your life at the moment?

Chapter Fifteen

1. Why is the theophanic appearance of God as an African American woman disturbing to some? Why is it enriching to others? Why is it important for Mack?
2. At root, what is Young seeking to communicate to us about God with this metaphor for God?
3. How does this theophany challenge or affirm the picture of God in our own hearts and minds?

Chapter Sixteen

1. How does Young's use of "Papa" impact you? What are the positives and negatives of this language?
2. What point does using "Papa" underscore for Young? Why is this important?
3. How would you describe your experience of intimacy with God? Use, for example, a single word to identify it.

Chapter Seventeen

1. Why is it important to steer a middle course between modalism and tritheism? What are those two ideologies, and why are they problematic?
2. What do you think is the significance of Papa's wounds? Why is this important for the relationship within the Trinity as well as God's relationship with us?

Chapter Eighteen

1. What is the real heart of Young's depiction of the Trinity? Why is this important for wounded people?
2. Define "*perichoresis*." How does this open up the significance of the Trinity for many?

Chapter Nineteen

1. What is appealing and/or unappealing about Young's metaphor for the Holy Spirit?
2. What does the Spirit do for Mack? How is the Spirit a healer for Mack's wounds?
3. How do you experience the work of the Spirit in your own life?

Chapter Twenty

1. What does it mean to say Jesus lived as a fully dependent, limited human being? Why is this important? How does it connect with our own experience?

2. How does Jesus model intimacy with God even as he lives as a dependent, limited human being?

3. Is Jesus forever human? How does that thought enrich your love and appreciation for what God has done?

Chapter Twenty-One

1. Why do we feel the need to defend or justify God? Can we really do that? What are our limitations in such a venture?

2. How are "lament or protest" as well as "actions" a response to suffering in the world?

3. Why must trust be our fundamental response in the search for answers? What does that mean? Are there any other viable options?

Chapter Twenty-Two

1. Why do some cringe when someone quotes Romans 8:28 in response to suffering? How have you heard this text abused?

2. What do you think about this statement: "Everything that happens serves the Grand Purpose of God within the Grand Story God is authoring"? What does that mean? What problems arise when we are thinking about that statement?

3. How are the dark spots in a tapestry part of its beauty? Is this true about life as well?

Chapter Twenty-Three

1. What are some of the names that have scarred, wounded, or shamed you? How have you named yourself?

2. What are God's names for you? How do we learn to "feel" these in our gut so we are truly renamed and transformed?

Chapter Twenty-Four

1. Why is it difficult to believe God loves us just as he loved Jesus?

2. How do we learn to embrace and feel this truth so that it shapes our identity?

Chapter Twenty-Five

1. What are your greatest fears? How are these fears debilitating?

2. Why is trust so difficult in the face of such fear?

3. How is trust developed and deepened in our walk with God?

Chapter Twenty-Six

1. What are the roots of mourning in your life? What saps life from you?

2. Where do you find joy in life? What gives you life?

3. What is our greatest fear, according to Young? Do you agree?

4. What is life like when we are convinced that God deeply loves us?

Study Plans

13-Week Study Plan
Week 1 – Introduction and Chapter 1
Week 2 – Chapters 2 & 3
Week 3 – Chapters 4 & 7
Week 4 – Chapters 5 & 6
Week 5 – Chapters 9 & 10
Week 6 – Chapters 11 & 12
Week 7 – Chapters 8 & 13
Week 8 – Chapters 14 & 15
Week 9 – Chapters 16 & 17
Week 10 – Chapters 18 & 19
Week 11 – Chapters 20 & 21
Week 12 – Chapters 22 & 23
Week 13 – Chapters 24 & 25

6-Week Study Plan
Week 1 – Introduction – Chapter 3
Week 2 – Chapters 4–7, 13
Week 3 – Chapters 8–12
Week 4 – Chapters 14–17
Week 5 – Chapters 18–21
Week 6 – Chapters 22–25

4-Week Study Plan
Week 1 – Introduction – Chapter 7
Week 2 – Chapters 8–13
Week 3 – Chapters 14–19
Week 4 – Chapters 20–25

CPSIA information can be obtained
at www.ICGtesting.com
Printed in the USA
FFOW05n0754140417